Fifty Hikes in Northern Maine

Walks, Day Hikes, and Backpacks
in the Northern Mountains and Lake Country

Cloe Caputo

Photographs by the autho

A Fifty Hikes™ Guide

Backcountry Publications
The Countryman Press, Inc.
Woodstock, Vermont

For Ian, Skye, Curry, and Cory

An Invitation to the Reader

Over time trails can be rerouted and signs and landmarks altered. If you find that changes have occurred on the routes described in this book, please let us know so that corrections may be made in future editions. The author and publisher also welcome other comments and suggestions. Address all correspondence to:

Editor
Fifty Hikes™ Series
Backcountry Publications
P.O. Box 175
Woodstock, Vermont 05091

Library of Congress Cataloging-in Publication Data

Caputo, Cloe, 1947–
    Fifty hikes in northern Maine: walks, day hikes, and backpacks in the northern mountains and lake country / Cloe Caputo; photographs by the author.
      p.   cm.
    "A Fifty hikes guide."
    ISBN 0–88150–129–8: $10.95
    1. Hiking—Maine—Guide-books. 2. Backpacking—Maine—Guide -books. 3. Trails—Maine—Guide-books. 4. Maine—Description and travel—1981- —Guide-books. I. Title. II. Title: 50 hikes in northern Maine.
    GV199.42.M2C36   1989
    917.41—dc20   89–32131
                                                     CIP

Published by Backcountry Publications
A division of The Countryman Press, Inc.
Woodstock, Vermont 05091

Printed in the United States of America
Typesetting by Sant Bani Press
Series design by Wladislaw Finne
Trail overlays by Richard Widhu

Photograph on page 161 by Joe Caputo
Photographs on pages 11 and 39 by Larry Catlett
Photograph on page 37 by Lorraine Hart
Photographs on pages 107, 129, 191 by Marc Johnson
Photographs on pages 94 and 162 by Dave O'Connor
Cover photographs and all other photographs by the author
Frontispiece: The Owl and Mount Katahdin

Acknowledgments

Without the help of some important people, this book would not have been as fun to write and the result would have been less than it is. I would like to thank Buzz Caverly, Steve Clark, Wayne Ferland, John Gibson, Lorraine Hart, Herb Hartman, Jean Hoekwater, Lester Kenway, Ken Lee, Jeanie Levitan, Jon Lund, Jane McGraw, Joan Benoit Samuelson, Joyce Schweback, Carl Taylor, and Don Varney for their contributions, hard work, and valuable assistance. And special thanks to my husband and hiking companion, Joe Caputo.

Contents

Introduction

Anywhere in Maine, hiking is a pleasure. In many places, it is also a challenge. The hikes and backpacking trips in this guide range from easy strolls to strenuous climbs. Some will be very popular, and on some, you might not encounter anyone else.

Of the fifty hikes, forty-six are day hikes and have been grouped into geographical sections. Each section offers a variety of hikes, from easy to difficult. Some are appropriate for getting into shape or for hiking with infants and young children. Many more offer a challenge to the hiker because of length, vertical rise, or ruggedness. You can estimate a hike's difficulty from the distance and vertical rise given at the beginning of each hike, as well as from the hike description. A seventh section contains four two- to five-day-long backpacking trips. These four backpacking trips—two in the western Maine mountains near Rangeley Lake and two in Baxter State Park—require that you be in good physical condition.

Maine Trails

The trails described here are a sampling of those found in the northern and western parts of the state, up mountains, to waterfalls, and through prime timberland. I have included hikes in the North Maine Woods, in Baxter State Park, and through holdings of The Nature Conservancy. Some trails incorporate sections of Maine's 280-mile-long stretch of the Appalachian Trail, and others traverse the state-owned Bigelow Preserve. On many trails, hikers are the guests of timber, pulp, and land companies: Scott, International, Boise Cascade, Great Northern, Seven Islands, Georgia-Pacific, St. Regis, Diamond, Oxford, Brown, and Dead River. A few hikes cross the private property of individuals. Regardless of ownership, all land deserves our utmost respect.

Maine's trails are always changing. Firetower trails become overgrown when towers are abandoned. Sometimes sufficient use maintains a trail; sometimes new trails are cut and maintained. Logging operations construct many new dirt roads in the deep forest each year, while numerous other old roads are in some stage of returning to forest. This dynamic aspect of Maine's woods roads and trails means that road approaches and the terrain you will hike may vary from the hike descriptions in this guidebook. These changing conditions are the most important reason for carrying topographical maps: manmade features and even forest cover alter, but land contours, streams, ponds, and compass directions rarely change. Whenever possible, you should confirm hiking directions locally.

Total Distance, Hiking Time, Vertical Rise, and Maps

Each hike description begins with a summary of total distance, hiking time, and vertical rise. These figures should help you judge the hike's difficulty and decide if a hike is within the limits of your ability and the amount of time you have to spend on the trial.

Total distance is the total number of miles you will hike on the suggested trails. Each hike description clearly indicates if this distance refers to a circuit or loop, a return by the same route, or a one-way hike (where cars are spotted at both the beginning and end of the trail). If side trails to sites of interest are included in the totals, this fact is noted in the hike description.

Hiking time includes all time spent walking or climbing but does not include time for resting, picnicking, swimming, or simply enjoying the view. Times given are for a leisurely but steady pace, allowing for differences in terrain. If you pursue an alternate or side trail that is not included in the total distance, remember to adjust your hiking time also. Allow yourself enough time for the special attractions of a hike, as well as enough time to cover the ground.

Vertical rise is the total distance climbed upward on a hike. The vertical rise may be more than the total gain in elevation if a trail often repeats an up-and-down pattern. On many hikes, especially strenuous ones, I have tried to indicate where along the trail you gain particularly significant amounts of the vertical rise.

In general, a difficult hike has a greater amount of vertical rise per mile, a longer total distance, and a longer hiking time than an easier hike. The vertical rise per mile is usually the best clue about how challenging a hike is.

Maps are suggested in each hike heading so that you can obtain supplements to the ones in this guide. The maps that accompany the hike descriptions are based on the appropriate United States Geological Survey (USGS) topographical sheets. Some of the areas hiked have USGS maps available in both 7.5′ and 15′ series. When both options are available we have listed the quadrangle names for each. The maps in this book give a good general idea of the trails followed but are less helpful if you are lost because, of necessity, they show less area than the originals on which they are based. It is always a good idea to carry USGS maps with you, both for a safer trip and for educational purposes. When using these maps, however, bear in mind that although land features remain relatively constant, the area may have been surveyed and mapped before the trail was cut, or the trail may have been relocated. The USGS maps, as well as a state index, price list, and pamphlet describing how to read the maps, can be obtained directly from the government by writing to: Distribution Branch, US Geological Survey, Box 25286, Federal Center, Denver, CO 80225 (303–236–7477). The maps are also available at many sporting goods stores.

Maps other than the USGS sheets are sometimes listed in the summary headings. The Baxter Park Map refers to the free map you receive when you enter one of the Baxter State Park gates. It can also be obtained in advance when you make reservations. Steve Clark's detailed map and guidebook for Baxter Park can also be purchased at Park Headquarters, 64 Balsam Drive, Millinocket, ME 04462 (207-723-5140).

The *North Maine Woods Map* referred to in hikes in the Moosehead region and Aroostook County is available for $2.00 postpaid from an association of paper, timber, and land companies by writing to: North Maine Woods, Inc., PO Box 421, Ashland, ME 04732-0421.

And finally, the MATC maps refer to

First aid for a blister

the strip maps published by the Maine Chapter of the Appalachian Trail Conference and included in their *Guide to the Appalachian Trail in Maine.* You can obtain this guide with its seven strip maps by writing to the Maine Appalachian Trail Club, Inc., Box 283, Augusta, ME 04330. This organization will also provide other information on hiking in Maine. The Appalachian Trail (AT) has gone through extensive changes in the last ten years as both the National and Maine ATC have worked to achieve complete protection and have routed the trail away from roads as much as possible. Therefore, older AT maps and guides are of no use for many hikes now. The 1988 edition is up-to-date and will probably remain so indefinitely, for the trail is now stabilized for, we hope, a

long while. This book refers to the 1988 edition, which is the only edition that should be used.

Clothing and Equipment

Because many of these hikes are not heavily traveled, you should be especially prepared with your own first aid, warm clothing, rain gear, fire-starting equipment, food, and maps. A compass and this guidebook (or a photocopy of the hike you are following) should always be carried. Most trails are well marked and easy to follow, but on some of the rougher trails a compass is important for interpreting book directions.

When giving compass bearings, I have adjusted my compass for the declination appropriate for each hike. Declination is the difference between magnetic and true north. Maine's declination varies from 17 to 22 degrees, usually around 20 degrees for hikes in this book. To adjust your compass for the declination, rotate the compass so that north is 20 degrees to the right of the magnetic needle. Thus, the needle points to 340 degrees instead of 0 degrees, north.

Arranged in this way, the needle points, as always, to magnetic north, while the N points to true north, the north referred to in the book and designated on maps. Although the maps in this book are detailed, they can't show every twist and turn of the trail. The combination of landmarks, trail distances, and compass bearings at key points in the hike description should keep you on track.

For clothing, comfortable walking shoes should be your first consideration. Many of today's athletic shoes are sufficient for hiking and have the advantage of being light weight. Sturdy walking shoes or vibram-soled hiking boots are also desirable. Hiking in spring or after heavy rains sometimes calls for waterproof boots. Winter hiking demands insulated boots. Most important are fit and comfort.

For socks, wool is best, summer and winter. Wool does not absorb moisture and therefore does not lose its ability to cushion your feet. This is especially important in winter, when moisture will chill your feet quickly.

Other clothing choices are a matter of personal taste and your experience, as long as you carry enough. A rain jacket is necessary. In high winds, it can double as a wind shell for short periods. You should always tuck away a wool hat, mittens, and a wool sweater or shirt for unpredictable cold snaps and for use if you will be hiking above treeline. On a few hikes I suggest long pants. Otherwise, follow your own preference. Comfort should be the key.

Choose a rucksack or day pack large enough to hold your gear. Other pack items include matches in a waterproof holder, a knife, insect repellent, and a canteen and cup. A flashlight and a small first-aid kit with moleskin added should be tucked away. Your compass should be accessible. In addition to your lunch and snacks, you should carry spare food for two meals. Many people enjoy taking a camera or fishing rod and license along.

Backpackers will need a sleeping bag, foam pad, cooking utensils, matches (preferably the wind-proof type), and usually a tent and small stove. Supermarkets stock a variety of dehydrated foods. The backpack should be framed inside or out, should fit well, and have a sturdy waist or hip belt.

Observing and learning about nature can enhance a hiking trip, so I suggest you also pack one or two field guides.

Safety

Maine weather is unpredictable. Always use caution. This is crucial above treeline, where weather changes suddenly and drastically, and where there may be no place to go for shelter. If you want to hike in bad weather, choose a forest trail to a pond, waterfall, or wooded mountain.

Winter is a time to use special caution. Snowshoe and ski travel require much more time than summer hiking, and days are shorter. Weather can change quickly. In general, choose shorter hikes with minimum vertical rise. Some hikes will be inaccessible by road in winter. When a trail is particularly good for winter hiking or cross-country skiing, I have noted that in the hike description.

Before setting out, study maps and guidebooks. Estimate time needed for driving, hiking, eating, photography, and other activities. Inform a responsible person of your plans, where you will park your car, and when you expect to return. Carry a compass and enough emergency food and clothing so you can spend a night in the woods if necessary.

Getting lost happens to even the best of hikers. If you think you may be lost, the first step is to sit down and think rationally. You will probably remember where you missed the trail or took the wrong turn. Study your map and orient it with your compass. If you can figure out where you are, then you can find out where you meant to be. When you are really confused, find a stream to follow (downstream). If injured, build a fire if you can. Throw on green leaves and ferns as a smoke signal. And remember, if you left your itinerary with someone and you don't return when you are expected, someone will begin to search for you. For that reason, stick to your planned itinerary.

Drinking Water

Increasingly we hear about the illness giardiasis that afflicts hikers and campers who have used water from a stream for drinking or washing dishes. Although I have not heard of any cases in Maine, in Wyoming and other wild areas it has been known to make hikers terribly ill, either within a week of the hike or many months later.

Giardiasis is an infection of *Giardia lamblia,* a protozoan carried in human or animal feces that can infest fresh water. Unfortunately, you never know if a *Giardia*-carrying animal has contaminated the water upstream. Beavers are often the culprits. A spring (source of groundwater) is usually pure and much safer than surface water (streams, lakes). The size of the spring (the smaller the better) and its location determine its safety. If it issues from a cleaved rock or falls from an inaccessible source, it is probably safe. But beware of surface water of all types. Symptoms of giardiasis include severe diarrhea, nausea, and chills, which can last several days or weeks. If you should have these symptoms, see a doctor immediately for antibiotic treatment.

The best way to avoid *Giardia* is to carry water from home or a known safe source. As this is not always possible or practical, the National Park Service recommends boiling drinking or dish water for one minute, or using a filter for particles as small as one micron. Don't be misled by "granular charcoal" or "EPA registered" filters. Look for the filter size. They start at about $35. So far, the National Park Service does not recommend treatment with iodine tablets, as their effectiveness has not been proved.

Accommodations

Campgrounds and other accommodations are mentioned in the introduction to each section. Many, but not all, of the

On the Bigelow Range Trail

state parks offer overnight camping. To find out in advance, write to the Bureau of Parks and Recreation, State House Station 22, Augusta, ME 04333.

There is also a network of wilderness campsites approved and operated by the Maine Forest Service (MFS). The locations of these campsites are indicated in the DeLorme *Maine Atlas and Gazetteer* by the symbol for "maintained forest campsites"; the DeLorme atlas is available from the DeLorme Mapping Company, PO Box 298, Freeport, ME 04032. Remote areas have many MFS campsites located singly or two at a location. MFS sites permit fires in the proper fireplaces, are convenient to water, and usually have picnic tables. A very small fee is charged.

Respect for the Land

Rules and regulations are based on simple respect for land and property. Build fires only in authorized campsites; otherwise use a backpacking stove. If you camp in other than an authorized campsite, be sure to ask permission. In all cases, leave no sign that you were there. Trash should be carried out, not buried. Bodily waste should be buried at least 200 feet from any stream, spring, pond, or trail.

The various parks and forests have regulations of their own. Be familiar with them when you enter. By all means, be gentle with mother earth. She is our only home, a fact that many people seem to ignore.

Taking Children Along

Children are natural hikers for they have limited needs, and all outdoors is a toy to them. They are also easy to backpack when they are small.

In all hiking, the number one killer is a bad attitude. This single force is more powerful than bad weather, insects, heat, cold, getting lost, or a host of small inconveniences. When you are planning a hike with children, a few things to keep in mind will help your family preserve this good attitude.

Choose hikes with reasonable distances and reasonable vertical rises for your family's abilities. When in doubt, try the easier rather than the more difficult hike. If you discover you have attempted a hike that becomes too difficult, adjust your plans. Shorten the hike or take it more slowly. Allowing your child to walk ahead of you sometimes makes a remarkable change in attitude and enthusiasm. But always keep your child in sight, whether ahead or behind you. Consider the ages of your children and how safe a trail is for them to walk or for you to hike while carrying them.

Babies up to two-years old are easy to pack. They love to be carried, can sleep in a backpack, and enjoy the rhythm of hiking. There are several commercial child carriers on the market. You should be careful to choose one with a waist or hip belt. (The belt transfers the load from your shoulders to your hips.)

Something I like even better is an old frame pack that has been converted into a child carrier. I cut and reinforced leg holes in the upper part of the pack bag, so the child sits in the top, facing backwards, and the rest of the pack's compartments can still hold cargo.

Two- and three-year olds can walk part of the way and ride part of the way. Four-year olds and older children can walk several miles if the pace is leisurely, and they enjoy carrying their own clothes, snacks, or lunch in a small pack. When a child is carried on an overnight trip, one adult needs to carry a pack with gear while another carries the child. Try to use lean-tos rather than tents whenever possible to lighten your load.

In general, spring, summer, and fall are the best seasons to hike with children. Clothing and equipment are heavier in winter hiking, and children can get very cold or wet before parents find out—they're slower to complain than adults.

Pace your hike with frequent rest and snack periods. High-energy snacks like dried fruits, granola, nuts, and raisins are children's favorites anyway, and they are lightweight and easy to pack. Carry plenty of water; children are almost *always* thirsty. Children under two need only a few simple modifications in food. Nursing babies are the most convenient —no food or bottles are necessary at all. Older babies need a bottle or cup for powdered milk and simple foods such as bananas, apples (shaved or scraped with a knife), and cheese. For longer trips, a small plastic food grinder adds little weight and allows the baby to share the parents' food.

Have changes of clothes, shoes, raincoat, hat, mittens, and a warm jacket for each child. Tuck plenty of extra socks in the child's pack. For some hikes, sneakers might be good enough, but others may require waterproof boots or sturdy hiking shoes. Take disposable diapers for babies, the kind that can be burned each day.

Children (and adults) will be happier with good bug protection. Use one of several good repellents and in hot weather, choose lightweight clothes that cover the whole body. A head screen can be made from a square yard of mosquito netting or other sheer material. Make a big circle by cutting the corners off the square. Turn under a small hem all around and run a piece of elastic throught the hem. The elastic should fit a small child comfortably around the waist (protecting the upper body and arms), and an adult or older child around the neck. A hat with brim will keep the netting away from your face.

Try to discourage children from bringing toys so they will notice the natural toys around them. Children love water, so it's a good idea to plan hikes with a swim or with other water features — falls, brooks, or ponds. Even a pot of water entertains a younger child. If children want to play in the rain, put their raincoats on them and let them play. If you are backpacking and fishing, your toddler will play with your catch of trout, put them to bed in the tent with washcloth covers, bathe them in a pan, and enjoy eating them for supper. Young children also need plenty of freedom as well as enough time to rest or nap. Older kids can learn to fish, practice orienteering (try a treasure hunt with compass and map or simple directions), experiment with photography, and help with camp chores. Remember that older children also need patient instruction in using a jackknife properly. Don't expect intuitive good sense or skill.

Help your children learn about nature by playing games with the objects of nature around you. Find hiding places, identify wildflowers or animal tracks, or collect leaves or rocks. Imagine which animals would pick which tiny trees for their Christmas trees, or use acorn cups and saucers, or float leaves down brooks. The number of items that can be made from the large leaves of striped maple is astonishing.

Planning for your family's safety and comfort should help children learn to enjoy, not detest, hiking. And as you try to interest your children in nature, you will find that their fresh outlook and unflagging curiosity will renew *your* interest in nature. You may recall the first time you stared into a bird's nest of tiny eggs, or saw a butterfly up close, or a deer track. Wildlife sightings are much more exciting and memorable with children along. Wildflowers, too, are dear friends; it's easy to teach a child to stoop down to smell the flowers instead of picking them. Sunsets, mountains, toads and frogs, birds catching insects, woodpeckers pecking, waterfalls and tiny brooks are all exciting for youngsters, as they should be for us. In the half hour it sometimes takes to get from here to twenty paces over there, we are reminded of the reasons we hike; what we lose in expectations of distance and accomplishment, we are repaid in enjoyment.

Key to Map Symbols

—— main trail

- - - side trail

A Appalachian Trail

Δ campground

⇥ lookout

Ⓟ parking

⋔ shelter

〰 brook

o o oo stone wall

—·—• dirt road

⨅ gate

INTRODUCTION

The Mount Blue area is generally west of Farmington and just north of Rumford, occupying parts of Franklin and Oxford counties. Weld, at the junction of ME 156 and ME 142, is the nearest village to Mount Blue, Tumbledown, Little Jackson, and Bald mountains, while Byron on ME 17 and Andover on ME 5 are closest to Angel Falls and Old Blue. This area offers the earliest spring hiking in northern and western Maine, as well as the latest in fall, and provides the best winter access.

Weld and Byron are connected by the Byron Notch Road, locally called "Number Six" because it is located in Township 6. The gravel road is used by logging trucks, but it is wide, well maintained, and safe.

Mount Blue State Park in Weld offers access to beautiful Lake Webb and has excellent camping. Campsites are easy to obtain; no reservations are necessary. The only other place where campfires are allowed is in Tumbledown Field at the Little Jackson trailhead (see Hike 3) off the Byron Notch Road, but you must first obtain a fire permit from the Weld *Maine Forest Service (MFS) office* (207–585–2427) on ME 156 or the Weld General Store. Center Hill Picnic Area at Mount Blue State Park has a self-guiding nature trail that takes you to a dramatic outlook on Center Hill. The interesting information and the beautiful panorama are well worth the few minutes' walk.

The proprietors of the Weld General Store, Jerry and Dot Nering, are enthusiastic about hiking and can give you any trail information you might need. They also sell USGS topographic maps for the area. If you plan to hike in winter, the Nerings have suggested that you leave your itinerary with them at the store so that if you don't return when expected, they can send help.

While at the store, you may also want to ask about directions and trail conditions for Blueberry Mountain, just a few miles up ME 142. Active logging operations have made the trail difficult to locate and to follow at the beginning. But with an update, you might be able to add this hike to the others described here for the Mount Blue area.

In Byron, be sure to stop at the Coos Canyon Rest Area at the junction of ME 17 and the Byron Notch Road from Weld. Coos Canyon is a beautiful series of falls and chutes through pools scoured and polished over millions of years. There is no camping in the immediate Byron area, but twenty miles north on ME 17 you will find the entrance road to Rangeley Lake State Park on beautiful Rangeley Lake. No reservations are necessary, for the park usually has vacancies.

1

Mount Blue

Total distance (round trip): 2.8 miles
Hiking time: 2½ hours
Vertical rise: 1,800 feet
Maps: USGS 7.5' Mount Blue; USGS 15' Dixfield

Mount Blue looks the way a mountain should. Seen from high on the ridge west of Lake Webb, it's an elegant picture—a memory you'll always associate with Maine. Blue's nearly perfect, cone-shaped mass rises like a gumdrop east of Lake Webb and south of Pope and Hurricane mountains. Mount Blue must be one of the most popular climbs in Maine, but, even on a summer day, the mountain is rarely crowded.

Head east from Weld on the paved road by the general store. Keep left at the first junction. The route shortly becomes a gravel road that winds eastward. Continue past the road (right) to Center Hill. Keep right at the next junction, arriving at a grassy parking area below the mountain about six miles from Weld. The road is well marked at all junctions.

From the parking area, you walk east-northeast up a grassy fire road, which very shortly enters the woods. The lower west ridge and the higher reaches of the mountain rise before you as you start up. Once in the woods, you climb sharply east and northeast up the ridge. This is steady, steep going by anyone's standards, but not difficult once you get your rhythm.

As you climb rapidly, you'll hear a brook off to the left. A short side path takes you to this source of water at about .7 mile. At 1 mile, you pass the fire warden's cabin on the left, where there is a spring, and swing steadily upward toward the northeast. The trail crests the north end of the lower ridge shortly, and you head east and southeast toward the summit. The grade becomes more comfortable for a short distance as you move toward the cone, but grows steep again as you turn nearly south for the final scramble to the top. Good views to the north and northwest begin to appear behind you here. The summit is reached at approximately 1.4 miles. The old fire tower is now loaded with microwave relay equipment complete with cold weather deicing heaters. It's rather an odd experience to stand on the upper levels of the tower, listening to the wind and the bleep, bleep, bleep of the relays inside.

A good deal of western Maine can be seen from Blue. Looking to the northeast, the 4,000-foot summit of Mt. Abraham (Hike 12) rises south of Black Nubble, Spaulding, and Sugarloaf mountains (Hike 48). Saddleback in Rangeley (Hike 11) can be seen almost due north. The other major summits of the Weld region are to the northwest, Tumbledown (Hike 2) and the Jacksons (Hike 3), while the imposing shapes of Baldpate and Old Speck in Grafton Notch rise to the southwest.

Geologically speaking, the bedrock of Mount Blue is a member of the Seboomook Formation, which is Devonian metamorphosed sandstones, slates, and schists. This formation is part of the regional "country rock" of the Franklin County area, explained in more detail in Hike 4, Bald Mountain. Although Mount Blue does not afford many opportunities to view its bedrock, since the trail and summit are wooded, the stones along the trail will give you an idea of what the underlying bedrock is like.

The neatly manicured circle of grass lawn on the summit of Blue is a helicopter landing pad. The two dozen or so tanks of propane used to run the microwave deicers are flown in periodically. Not very romantic, but it keeps the relays open. Head down the way you came up for a muscle-crimping, quick descent.

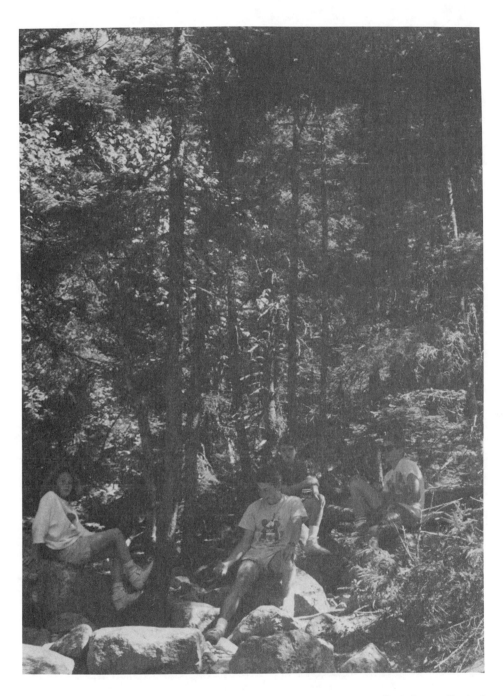

Rest stop on the trail

Tumbledown Mountain

Total distance (round trip): 5.5 miles
Hiking time: 4 hours
Vertical rise: 1,700 feet
Maps: USGS 7.5' Roxbury, Jackson Mountain; USGS 15'
  Rangeley, Rumford

Tumbledown, a three-peaked mountain, forms the northern border of Byron Notch. The mountain offers an excellent variety of climbing experiences. The Loop Trail to the summit will provide easy trail walking, steep climbing, some boulder scrambling, and even some hand-over-hand on the rock faces just below the summit. An interesting, little-bit-of-everything kind of mountain, this is the trip I use to get people hooked on hiking. It isn't as strenuous as Katahdin, and the experiences along the way are varied and exciting. And there is still trout fishing in Tumbledown Pond. Acid rain is beginning to affect this alpine tarn. Although it is not too acidic yet, if the trend continues, trout will no longer be able to live there.

To reach the trailhead, take the left (west) fork from ME 142 at Weld Corner, located about 2 miles north of Weld. Another fork is reached in 2.3 miles. Stay to the right here. The gravel road meanders past the entrance to the Parker Ridge Trail and the path to Little Jackson Mountain (Hike 3). Continue on and you'll reach the Chimney and Loop Trails on your right, just 3 miles beyond the Parker Ridge Trail sign. Stones and paint blazes mark the trail entrance. Park off the road to the left.

Your climb to Tumbledown's West summit begins from the north side of the Byron Notch Road, where you immediately enter the woods. You follow the blue blazes almost due north from the road, passing through young hardwoods and traversing nearly level ground. You quickly walk over a low ridge. The trail then meanders across a brook and down into a boggy area.

Turning northeast, you begin the real ascent of the ridge below Tumbledown Cliffs. You pass a balanced rock on a pedestal at about .5 mile, and a giant boulder at just under 1 mile. Tumbledown probably got its name from the giant boulder field you now climb.

The very steep ascent of the upper ridge will bring you, after a climb of about .3 mile, to the cairn where the Chimney Trail runs left and the Loop Trail goes to the right. Just below the cairn there are good outlooks to the south and west as you skirt the ledges. The old route to the West summit, the Chimney Trail, is no longer in use and should not be attempted. Rockfall at the top of the Chimney has made the area very dangerous and suitable only for those with rock-climbing skills. Turn right at the boulder, and head down through a depression to the east and northeast.

After passing through the depression, the trail climbs steeply north over and through boulders to the ridge between Tumbledown's West and East summits. Upon reaching the ridgeline, head left toward the West summit. The views here are fairly open toward the southeast over Lake Webb, Byron Notch, and surrounding hills. From the West summit, you can see Brush, West, and Walker mountains ranging southward across the Notch.

Tumbledown and the Jacksons are part of the Smalls Falls Formation, which is Silurian metamorphosed sandstones and schists. This formation is part of the "country rock" of the Franklin County area, described in more detail in Hike 4, Bald Mountain. At the exposed summit you can see veins of quartz that filled cracks that formed when these mountains were thrust up, either by compressive buckling, by granite welling up from underground, or by a combination of both during the Silurian period 390 to 430 million years ago. It would be interesting to see what is inside this mountain!

Monolith on the Tumbledown trail

Turning toward the east again, you retrace your steps along the ridge, pass the trail you ascended, and continue to the East summit. Here you'll find beautiful, little Tumbledown Pond, nestling in the col between Tumbledown and Little Jackson mountains. The best views are just above the pond, and there are good spots to sit and have your lunch down by the water. From the pond you can also walk down the mountain via the Parker Ridge Trail (see map), which heads northeast over Parker Ridge. This trail will bring you out to Byron Notch Road 3 miles east of your car.

Your descent via the Brook Trail begins at the outlet, at the southeast edge of Tumbledown Pond. Tricolor Timberlands blazes lead you down, crisscrossing the brook. Don't take any side trails. Stay with the blazes along Tumbledown Brook, which, by the way, is sometimes panned for gold. The trail is steep and requires careful footing until it eases onto an old logging road, still following the brook. About 1.5 miles down from the pond's outlet, the trail ends at the Byron Notch Road. Turn right and walk 1.4 miles on the road to your car at the Loop trailhead.

Little Jackson Mountain

Total distance (round trip): 6 miles
Hiking time: 5 hours
Vertical rise: 1,800 feet
Maps: USGS 7.5' Roxbury, Jackson Mountain; USGS 15'
  Rangeley, Rumford

The trail for Little Jackson Mountain is reached via the Byron Notch Road from Weld corner. Take the left (west) fork at Weld Corner about 2 miles north of Weld on ME 142. You come to another fork at 2.3 miles. Stay to the right here. The gravel road shortly reaches the entrance to the Parker Ridge Trail and the path to Little Jackson Mountain. Both trails initially follow a gravel road leading past a camping area with plenty of room for parking. This camping area, called "Tumbledown Field," is the only place an open campfire is permitted, but a fire permit must be obtained from the Maine Forest Service (MFS) station in Weld (207–585–2427) or from the Weld General Store. The road ends at a shelter where the Parker Ridge trail runs left and west, while the trail to Little Jackson runs right up a logging road.

Walk up the logging road through a luxuriant growth of wild berries. You are headed north and northwest. In .3 mile you pass through a large clearing once used for loading logs. At a fork a little beyond the clearing, keep right, climbing steadily due north. Watch for faded paint blazes on the rocky way. Behind you views of the valley can be seen.

You reach a second fork .2 mile above the clearing. Bear left here at an orange painted arrow. (The rocky logging road continues to the right.) After you pass a small, grown-up meadow —with views across the notch to Spruce Mountain behind you—your ascent grows steeper on a narrow path. Moose may be encountered here. The path, after being heavily overgrown with grass, shortly becomes rocky again and continues to rise steeply northward toward the col between Little and Big Jackson mountains.

Be sure to avoid the many small, unused logging roads that meander off the main path. There are enough of them to confuse a saint. You climb up through spruce and fir, rising above the hardwood groves. Follow the arrows briefly west, then just as briefly north and northeast. The path enters a closely wooded section where birches and young beech parallel the pathway at approximately 1.5 miles from the trailhead. You slab the extreme southwest ridge of Big Jackson for a short distance as you approach the col between the two peaks. A brook is crossed just below the col, at about 2.3 miles.

After crossing the brook, you run briefly west and then north again through fine stands of brilliant white birch. The trail levels off momentarily and then climbs very steeply to the high point of the col on open ledges, offering fine views of the surrounding peaks.

Traveling briefly north to a prominent cairn, you then turn west for the summit. The trail is not well marked, and painted blazes must be carefully hunted out. The route wanders erratically southwest and south from the col, reaching the summit in about .7 mile.

Looking east to Little Jackson and Big Jackson from Tumbledown summit

The excellent north-south views from the col are improved upon by the outlook from Little Jackson's summit. The Rangeley Lakes region is to the northwest, the imposing mass of Saddleback (Hike 11) is to the east of the lakes, and still more to the right, you'll see the outline of Sugarloaf (Hike 48). The trailless summit of Big Jackson is immediately to the east with the three peaks of Tumbledown (Hike 2) lying over Tum-bledown Pond to the southwest. Lake Webb shines below to the southeast.

When descending by the same route you followed in, watch carefully for the cairn on the col where the trail turns right and toward the south.

A description of local geology can be found in the texts of Hike 2, Tumbledown Mountain and Hike 4, Bald Mountain.

Bald Mountain (Weld)

Total distance (round trip): 3 miles
Hiking time: 1½ hours
Vertical rise: 1,400 feet
Maps: USGS 7.5′ Mount Blue; USGS 15′ Dixfield

To get a good look at Lake Webb and its surrounding mountains from the south, you've got to climb Bald Mountain, which lies between Weld and Wilton on ME 156. The mountain is in what is officially designated Perkins Township. Find the right destination on a road map before you set out. Remember, there are dozens of mountains in Maine designated bald.

This hike is short and relatively steep, but not too steep for most, from small children to Grandma. They will know they have accomplished something, but they will be able to make it.

The trail to the 2,386-foot summit begins on the south side of Route 156, just over 5 miles from Weld and little over 8 miles from Wilton, .2 mile south of the Perkins and Washington Township line. There is a small clearing here for parking. A narrow signpost indicates the trailhead, but the sign is often missing. Walking southwest from the road, you quickly cross a brook and proceed gradually up through mixed hardwoods on a fairly well-defined path. There are occasional blazes, but the trail bears close watching, particularly in its lowest section.

Climbing on a grade that is sometimes steep, you shortly emerge above the timberline into scrub and then onto the ledges. There is little protection from the elements above here on windy or stormy days, so dress accordingly, and if the weather gets really vicious—head down. Cairns mark the remainder of the route, which rises at a comfortable rate to the summit, 1.5 miles from the trailhead.

Cherry Hill is immediately to your west, while the peak to the southwest is the higher, second summit of Bald, now renamed Saddleback Wind. A poorly maintained trail leads to this peak, but as the going is rough, the walk is not recommended. Lakin Hill lies northeast of Cherry Hill, and you have a good view of Lake Webb between the two. Mount Blue with its tower (Hike 1) is due north over the waters of Hill Pond. Walker, West, and Brush mountains are visible some distance to the northwest beyond the lake. Tumbledown (Hike 2), the Jacksons (Hike 3), and Blueberry Mountain form the exceptionally beautiful north border of the area.

Bald Mountain is a granodiorite pluton, a mound of bedrock slightly darker than granite that welled up in molten form like a blister under the regional

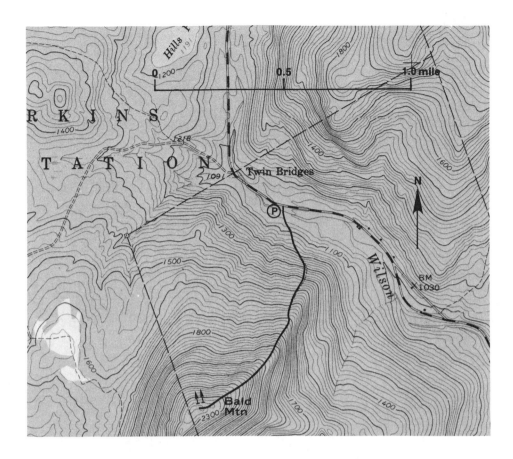

sedimentary rock that covered it. As it welled up, it heated and changed these overlying sedimentary layers into harder metamorphic rock, the surrounding "country rock" of slates and schists in this area. Solutions of quartz dissolved in water coursed through any cracks in the stretched layers over the blister, leaving veins of rock quartz when it cooled.

These metamorphic layers have begun to erode away from Bald Mountain, exposing its granodiorite interior at the summit. However, the climb begins on country rock, the metamorphic shell still covering the lower reaches of the moun-

tain. Examine the various stones in and along the trail. Some are chunks of granodiorite from above, and many are the metamorphic tailings that were clipped off by freeze-thaw actions and other weathering processes. Some of these metamorphic schist rocks contain staurolites, little cross-shaped minerals (or pieces of crosses) visible on the surface of the rock. These staurolites tell us about the nature of metamorphism in this region, its underground temperature and pressure during mountain-building around 350 million years ago.

In late May and early June you will discover ladyslippers shyly nestled

Bald Mountain behind Hills Pond

among rocks in the scrub growth of sheep laurel here and there over the broad summit.

It's an easy 35-minute walk down to the road from the summit. Take care not to miss the entry to the woods below the cairns on the return.

Angel Falls

Total distance: 1.25 miles
Hiking time: 1 hour
Vertical rise: 200 feet
Maps: USGS 7.5' Houghton; USGS 15' Oquossoc

Not often does a hike as rewarding as Angel Falls require so little effort. The 70-foot cascade rivals Moxie Falls (Hike 18) in the largest-single-drop-in-Maine category (both make the claim, and both deserve it!). Originally named Mountain Brook Falls for its location, it has also been called Lost Falls.

The trail is in Houghton, which can be approached from several directions. You can drive south from Oquossoc, 18 miles from the junction of ME 4 and ME 17; or you can drive north from Byron, 4.2 miles from the rest area at Coos Canyon, a beautiful canyon cut and polished by natural scouring, located to the right (east) of ME 17 at its junction with the Byron Notch Road to Weld. Byron can be approached from two different directions: north from Mexico on ME 17, or from Weld (ME 142) across the ten-mile, unpaved Byron Notch Road to Coos Canyon at ME 17.

From either of these approaches, look carefully for a dirt road to the west off ME 17 that immediately crosses a bridge over the Swift River. A state highway marker at this turn is numbered 6102. About .2 mile after you cross the bridge, a small sign lets you know you are in Houghton; fork right at this sign.

You are now driving on the old railroad bed that parallels Berdeen Stream northwest, with Brimstone Mountain ahead of you. Pass through a gate at 1.2 mile. At 2.5 miles from ME 17, pass a road to your left, and at 3.6 miles, turn left and park in a gravel pit. You may see a red "AF" sign at the turn.

The half-mile trail begins from the gravel pit. Ignore the road to the right and begin walking on the grassy road straight ahead, crossing a washed-out culvert. Just ahead, you rock-hop across Berdeen Stream, catching the pretty view in both directions. From here, the trail is marked with red wooden arrows and old red paint blazes on trees.

After crossing the stream, turn left and walk downstream about 100 yards to a small clearing where the trail divides, to the left along the stream, and to the right away from the stream. (You'll return by the trail on your left). Bear right, rising briefly to another clearing where the trail angles slightly to the right through mature hardwoods with some grand old beech and maples. The diminutive fern growing on the forest floor is oak fern, and the lacy fern in circlets is spinulose wood fern.

After a ten- to fifteen-minute walk from the gravel pit, the trail crosses a faint intersection a few yards before reaching Mountain Brook. (Remember this intersection because you will go back on the trail that joins you here.) A few paces take you to a big slab of rock overhanging Mountain Brook. From here, the rail zigzags across the brook several times, following red paint blazes on rocks. This is an inviting glen, cool even on a hot day, adorned with ferns and mosses. Even if there were no falls ahead, this stream would be well worth the drive and the walk.

About half an hour from the start, after a turn to the left, you pick your way through boulders to the base of Angel Falls. The 70-foot metamorphic wall of phyllites, slates, and schists rises vertically in pyramidal and polyhedral slabs, while wispy plumes of spray resembling angel hair fall from Mountain Brook

above. This is the end of the trail and a beautiful spot for lunch and a dip in the pool below the falls.

It is possible to scale the cliff left of the falls and to get a bird's-eye view down the falls, but extreme care should be taken, both for personal safety and to avoid erosion of the steep cliff. A short walk above takes you past smaller cataracts. If you stop to picnic or climb to the top of the falls, you should lengthen the expected hiking time of this walk.

Waterfalls can result from a number of conditions usually associated with certain rocks or rock types being harder than an adjacent rock type in a stream. At the top of the falls, the metamorphosed sedimentary bedrock appears to have been tilted on its side during a folding event, heaving its bedding planes from their horizontal position when sedimented to a nearly vertical ori-

Angel Falls

entation. This vertical bedding position could account for the erosion-resistant quality of the bedrock at this point in the stream, adjacent to the steeply cut waterfall below it.

On the return trip to your car, begin by backtracking along the stream. When you've crossed it for the last time, watch for the trail intersection just into the woods. Instead of walking straight ahead on the trail you came on, turn right, paralleling Mountain Brook downstream, although it is not in view much of the way. Follow the red arrows backwards, descending through yellow birch and maple in open sunny woods. From the intersection, it is .5 mile to your car at the gravel pit, and you will cross Berdeen Stream at the same ford.

Old Blue and Clearwater Brook

Total distance: 10 miles
Hiking time: 7 hours
Vertical rise: 2,300 feet
Maps: USGS 7.5' Andover, Metallak Mountain; USGS 15' Old
* Speck Mountain, Oquossoc; MATC 7 (1988)*

Old Blue, in the heart of the western Maine mountains near Andover, was trailless until 1979 when the Appalachian Trail (AT) was relocated over its summit. Before the relocation, few people climbed Old Blue as it had the reputation for being a tedious bushwhack. At 3,600 feet, it missed the "Hundred Highest" list by a few feet, so it was never a quarry for peak baggers, who might have found the thick undergrowth a challenge. Consequently, this fine peak is, for a time, unspoiled by hordes of humans.

The land you will hike is owned by the International Paper Company, the Brown Company, and Seven Islands Land Company. The Bates College Outing Club worked for two years clearing and preparing this 4½-mile-long relocation. Because the new section meets the old AT, now called the Clearwater Brook Trail, at the northern end of the mountain, this is one peak you can explore without having to backtrack.

Although also very enjoyable in spring and summer, this hike is especially scenic in fall, for it takes you up through mixed hardwoods, some very old, through spruce on Old Blue's summit, and back down the Clearwater Brook

Trail through large mixed hard-woods. Except for the all-spruce summit, there is plenty of birch, maple, and other hardwood color, with some interesting fall wildflowers underneath. Since water is available only from brooks, you should take full canteens with you.

To get to the trailhead, travel US 2 to Rumford Point, west of Rumford, where you bear right (north) on ME 5 to Andover. Continue north 8.5 miles from the four corners in Andover on the road to South Arm, taking left turns at .5 mile and at 3.2 miles. The white blazes of the AT and the trail sign can be seen where the trail crosses ME 5 deep in Black Brook Notch.

The trail leaves the road to the northeast, climbing steeply up the northeast side of Black Brook Notch. The first .6 mile rises over shelves of yarrow, asters, and other flowers, gaining 900 feet, which makes it one of the steepest sections of the AT in Maine. However, you soon reach the top of a cliff, after which the ascent is more gentle. While you catch your breath, the cliff offers views southwest to Sawyer Mountain with Moody Mountain behind, both of which are on another recent relocation of the AT on the way to the Hall Mountain lean-to. Southeast over Ellis Pond stands the white globe of the Andover Telstar Tracking Station.

From here the trail rises more gradually through mixed spruce and hardwoods, some trees very old and large with big burls. Beneath you is typical hardwood ground cover: wild sarsaparilla, ferns, asters, red berries of hobblebush and Solomon's plume (false Solomon's seal), and blue beads of clintonia lily. Especially interesting is the doll's-eye (white baneberry) — low plants with maplelike leaves whose spring white flowers turn in fall to white berries with a black dot, resembling a doll's eye with black pupil.

You rise over four wooded knobs or "false summits," mounting the southwest shoulder of Old Blue. At the base of the main dome of the mountain, begin the 800-foot climb of the southwest slope, rising through spruce-fir duff and then sheep laurel, mountain-ash, bunchberry, and scrub spruce to the open white granite summit. The 360-degree view is one of the best in western Maine: north to the two humps of Elephant Mountain with Bemis Mountain (Hike 47) behind, east to peaky Tumbledown (Hike 2) with Mount Blue (Hike 1) behind, southeast to Ellis Pond with Telstar behind, southwest to Baldpate, and beyond, Old Speck, the third highest peak in Maine. To the west over the west peak of Old Blue lie the Richardson Lakes and Pond-in-the-river (Rapid River).

From the summit, descend steeply at first and then gradually over soft ground through spruce-balsam woods. The further you go, the bigger the trees become. Cross a spring brook and enter a virgin forest of huge red spruce. Here you will reach a junction where the relocation ends. (The AT continues to the right to Elephant Mountain.) Turn left onto the former AT, its blazes now painted blue as the Clearwater Brook Trail. In .3 mile, as you begin crossing and recrossing the headwaters of Clearwater Brook, the hardwoods, including some cherry trees, begin to return.

Cross Clearwater Brook, now large, where there is a pool of water deep enough to submerge yourself. The trail follows the widening stream through birch woods populated with partridge here and there. After passing vertical chunks of stratified bedrock on your left, cross back to the north side of Clearwater Brook. You pass a lovely set of cascades into a pool flecked with iron pyrite glinting gold. The rocks are stained red, and the freezing water tastes of iron. The trail leaves the brook and follows an old woods road through beech and birch, bears right onto a dirt road for .5 mile, and runs back out onto ME 5.

Turn left and walk 2.3 miles along the road back to your car. While walking, you can trace your hike over Old Blue's skyline on your left. You will pass a couple of mammoth birches on the roadside, as well as the fleecy white down of fireweed in the fall, goldenrod, yarrow, joe-pye weed, and the red berries of mountain ash. If your party is large enough to have come in two cars, you can eliminate this last road stretch by spotting one of the cars where Clearwater Brook Trail meets ME 4, 2.3 miles from the trailhead.

INTRODUCTION

The Rangeley region is famous for its lakes of all sizes, its fly-fishing, re-
sorts, and downhill skiing. The town of Rangeley has restaurants, gift
shops, sporting goods, and lodgings of varying sophistication. Between
ME 17 and ME 4 on the south shore of Rangeley Lake, the state park is
a good place for camping and recreation. No reservations are necessary, for the park usually has vacancies.

The drive up ME 17 from Rumford and Byron offers stunning views
west over Mooselookmeguntic Lake of the western Maine and New
Hampshire mountains. Sunsets are particularly thrilling from Height-of-
the-Land, where the Appalachian Trail crosses the highway. Farther
north, there are dramatic views east over Rangeley Lake of Saddleback,
Sugarloaf, and Bigelow in the "4000 Footers" stretch of the Appalachian
Trail.

Here in northern Franklin and Oxford counties you are also in snowmobile country, offering a vast network of well-groomed trails branching
to Canada. Saddleback is one of the best downhill ski areas in Maine,
offering many cross-country ski trails as well. The large lakes are a
mecca for fly-fishermen: the Richardson Lakes, Mooselookmeguntic,
Rangeley, Aziscoos, and Parmachenee.

Hiking can be easy and civilized in this area, as with Bald Mountain
on the peninsula separating Mooselookmeguntic and Rangeley Lakes,
or solitary in utter wilderness, as with West Kennebago and Aziscoos
mountains or Mount Abraham. The Sabbathday Pond Loop is flat and
interesting, while Mount Abraham is a climb of over 3000 vertical feet.
There's a hike for everybody in Rangeley.

7

Sabbathday Pond Loop

Total distance (around loop): 6 miles
Hiking time: 4½ hours
Vertical rise: 500 feet
Maps: USGS 7.5′ Houghton; USGS 15′ Rangeley; MATC 6
  (1988)

The hike in to Sabbathday Pond Shelter, along the shores of Long Pond, and back over Spruce Mountain will give you a chance to sample the serene beauty of the isolated Four Ponds area. This is not a demanding hike—it can be done in as little as four and one-half hours—and much of the walk is on level ground skirting Long Pond. The loop makes an excellent day hike, with a pause at the shelter for lunch. It is also a good winter hike, either for the day or for overnight if your sleeping bags are rated for the temperatures expected.

Rest stop on Four Ponds Brook

You can travel on cross-country skis or snowshoes, but allow six to seven hours for the trek.

The trailhead is located on ME 17, 11.8 miles south of Oquossoc and .6 mile south of the Appalachian Trail (AT). The trail crossing is well marked, and there is parking on the east side of the road. Your route begins on the east side of the road opposite the Bemis Stream Trail sign. This route used to be the Appalachian Trail. It is now an unmarked path that runs east toward the Four Ponds and is easily followed.

From the highway, you proceed eastward on what remains of an old tote road just to the right of Four Ponds Brook. The trail rises only slightly as you meander through groves of red and

black spruce. The path follows the brook closely here, and there are some pretty rapids in high water.

The trail continues to the northeast and gradually moves around to the north-northeast, running on slight grades through fir and silver and white birch. About .3 mile into the woods, the trail pulls more to the right, toward the east and away from the brook. The path becomes wider as it runs again on a more pronounced old roadbed, climbing slightly along red spruce stands and lush clumps of spinulose wood fern. A small brook is crossed at just under 1 mile from the road, and the trail rejoins the banks of Four Ponds Brook at a dilapidated footbridge 1.2 miles from the road.

The trail *does not* cross the brook but pulls away to the right again on flat terrain, where the west shore of Long Pond soon comes into view through the trees. The ground is usually boggy and wet in this area.

You next proceed along the shore of Long Pond through groves of mature spruce on an extension of the old tote road you followed earlier. Another rutted tote road is shortly crossed at right angles as you continue east-southeast. Several of the Long Pond camps and a feeder brook are passed, and you soon move through a fine grove of young white birch. The path crosses the boggy isthmus of land between Long and Sabbathday ponds. Two and one-half miles from ME 17, you arrive at Sabbathday Pond Shelter in a small clearing.

Sabbathday, a small, kidney-shaped lake, makes a pretty sight from the lean-to. This is a good place to rest for lunch or for overnighting, but in high summer arrive early if you plan to camp. Additional tent platforms have been built behind the shelter in recent years, but, due to increased traffic on the Appalachian Trail in July and August, sleeping space here is at a premium.

From the shelter, you walk north over a slight rise toward Long Pond. The trail soon bears to the right and runs eastward along the shore of the pond. A sandy beach is passed in about .2 mile, after which the trail begins a gradual ascent to a pair of beaver bogs, bearing left and north-northwest between the bogs.

Three miles from ME 17, you pass over Bates Ledge in the shadow of Four Ponds Mountain, turning west. The route descends to a marshy area north of tiny Moxie Pond and then climbs gradually to the east summit of Spruce Mountain. You continue west and southwest to the west summit of the mountain, which though wooded, provides westward views through the trees to the Bemis Range. From Spruce's west summit, you make a sharp, quick descent to ME 17. The trail emerges opposite a scenic turnout with excellent views west toward Bemis Mountain and Mooselookmeguntic Lake.

To reach your car, turn left (south) on ME 17 and walk .6 mile to the parking area across from the Bemis Stream Trail.

Bald Mountain (Oquossoc)

Total distance (round trip): 2 miles
Hiking time: 1½ hours
Vertical rise: 950 feet
Maps: USGS 7.5' Oquossoc; USGS 15' Oquossoc

There's no better place to get the feel of the Rangeley Region than along the short trail up Bald Mountain, right in the midst of it all.

Although a low summit, Bald Mountain in Oquossoc provides some of the best lake views in Maine. Nestled on an arm of land between Rangeley Lake and Mooselookmeguntic Lake, Bald delivers a satisfying perspective on both the waterways of the area and the dozens of mountains that surround them.

To reach the trail, head west on ME 4 from Oquossoc. This little town, by the way, wasn't always quite so remote. It was once served by rail and was the jumping-off point for city folks or "sports" who had come to rough it in the many fine hostelries that formerly dotted the area. Both Stan Plummer, the stationmaster, and the trains are long gone, but the land around Oquossoc is still beautiful, as a climb on Bald will prove.

Slightly over 1 mile west of Oquossoc center, you reach Haines Landing. The road bears left and south and can be followed another 1 mile to the trail markers on the left side of the road, a short distance beyond the signs for Bald Mountain Camps. Park off the right-of-way.

The trail heads east from the road, and at first seems headed toward the ski slope on the north side of the mountain. Shortly you reach a fork. Keep to the right and proceed more southeasterly toward the summit. The trail rises steadily on comfortable grades with occasional views over your shoulder to Stoney Batter Point on Mooselookmeguntic Lake. The grade increases during the last .2 mile, as the trail makes the final pitch below the summit, 1 mile above the road.

To the northwest of your summit outlook lies Cupsuptic Lake, ranging north to Toothaker Brook. Immediately to the west are the upper reaches of Mooselookmeguntic and, farther west beyond Sandy Cove, the long, slender arc of Upper Richardson Lake. The Richardson Ponds and Aziscoos Lake (hidden from view by the hills north and east of Observatory Mountain) lie north of Upper Richardson. Student's Island and Toothaker Island are off the point of land to the south, with the extensive waters of Rangeley Lake stretching to the south-southeast.

This is certainly one of the finest lake and mountain viewpoints in Maine, and to attempt to praise it adequately would be about as futile as disinterestedly describing the fishing in the Richardson Ponds.

Bald Mountain is a knob of Ordovician

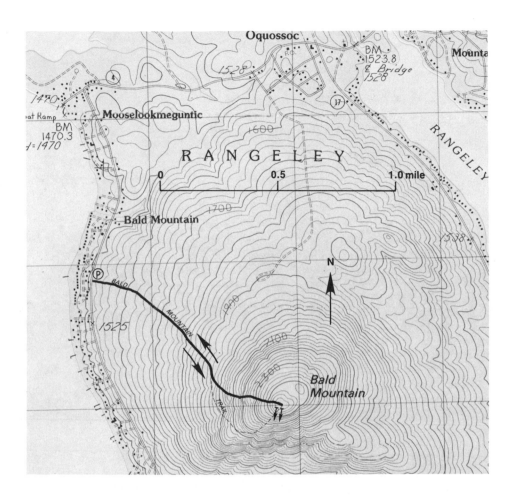

granite protruding from the surrounding "country rock" of metamorphic sandstones and schists. Its origins are thought to lie in a tectonic event that occurred 500 million years ago. At about this time, the North American tectonic plate collided with that of Europe and Asia, and the Appalachian Mountains were pushed up as wrinkles and corrugations, compressed between the continents. Our eastern seaboard was so corrugated and squeezed that molten magma from deep within the earth leaked out and oozed into the upper layers of the crust. This molten ooze formed blisters of granite, diorite, and gabbro under the "skin" or layers of sedimentary rock that had been laid down when Maine was covered by a shallow sea.

Some of the Appalachian mountains are purely corrugations of sedimentary rock, now metamorphosed by mountain-building temperatures and pressures. Others are blisters or plutons of granite (Bald Mountain, this hike), diorite (Saddleback Mountain, Hike 11), or gabbro (Sugarloaf, Hike 48) that cooled and

A rocky stretch on the trail

hardened over thousands of years underground. Some of these plutons have now been exposed by erosion. This is the case with Bald Mountain, a granite pluton that was exposed when the metasedimentary rock overlaying it was eroded away. We might well ask whether other mountains, like Bigelow, Tumbledown, and Abraham, hide similar granite, diorite, or gabbro plutons under their skins of slate, sandstone, or schist!

Return by the same trail.

Mount Aziscoos

Total distance (round trip): 3 miles
Hiking time: 3½ hours
Vertical rise: 1,700 feet
Maps: USGS 7.5′ Richardson Pond; USGS 15′ Oquossoc,
  Maine; USGS 15′ Errol, New Hampshire

The attractive Magalloway River rises in the highlands near the Quebec border in the northwest corner of Maine, feeds thirteen-mile-long Lake Aziscoos, and then flows over the dam near Wilson's Mills and on to the west and south.

South of the lake and east of the river rises Mount Aziscoos, a fine specimen of a mountain with outstanding water views. For those who keep score of such things, roughly fifteen lakes are visible from the summit of Mount Aziscoos when the weather is clear. Signs of the lumbering operations that took place here and there on the mountain in the early 1970s are now pretty much obscured by scrub, and most of Aziscoos remains densely forested and wild, with frequent signs of moose. Given its relatively isolated position west of Rangeley and Oquossoc, the mountain is never crowded, and it's rare to meet more than five or six people on the trail, even on a summer weekend. Aziscoos makes a good loner's mountain.

There were first two, then three trails up the mountain. The old route from the Aziscoos House up the west side of the rise is in disuse and grown up with brush. Another trail that climbs the mountain from the northwest just above the dam to the old fire warden's cabin, has also become rather hard to follow. A third trail, the most direct route to the summit from the north side of the mountain, is described here.

The trailhead is reached on ME 16 at a point 1 mile east of Aziscoos Dam and about 2.3 miles east of Wilson's Mills. The trail leaves the south side of the road by a good-sized turnout where there are small "Mount Aziscoos" signs on a tree. Once in the woods, you follow the remnants of an old tote road on easy grades to the south-southwest and southwest through a boggy area overgrown with spruce, young mountain ash, and a wealth of ferns: New York, sensitive, long beech, cinnamon, interrupted, and spinulose wood fern. In .2 mile, the route pulls more to the right briefly, running over spots of bald ledge

and through mixed growth.

Just under .5 mile from ME 16, the trail bears left onto another logging road after passing through a clearing. You continue south-southwestward here, in and out of the bed of the tote road, moving upward very gradually through stands of young beech and maple. Another more prominent logging road is crossed at right angles about .8 mile from the highway. You then begin a brisk ascent of a low ridge, moving south through clusters of birch and into a jumble of blowdown. The going is rough and the trail easily lost in this tangled spruce and balsam. At the time of this writing, the trail was blazed with red ribbon. Watch for these markers and telephone wire particularly in this section.

Rising steadily, you cross a brook at 1 mile. A hundred yards beyond the brook, a dead end branches off to the left. Take the right (main) trail following telephone wire and orange ribbons. There are views to the west here. The route continues upward and toward the south amidst stands of attractive fir and more scattered blowdown. As with most of the trail, scrub and brush overlay the path and the going is sometimes obscure. Red spruce branches in need of trimming narrow the trail and scratch the legs. Long pants would be nice for this one stretch, but regrettable for the rest of the hike if the weather is hot. At 1.4 miles from the trailhead, you reach a junction with an old trail from the northwest. Bear left or southeast and walk the remaining distance to the open east summit.

The broken remains of the fire warden's tower lie crumpled on the summit ledge. The bright mica-flecked granite is splotched with green lichen and dotted with blueberry bushes, sheep laurel, pin cherry, rhodora, and dwarfed spruce.

Aziscoos Mountain behind Aziscoos Lake dam

As always, nature is the best gardener! For me, it is sad to see so many Maine Forest Service towers left abandoned, especially ones like this, rusting on the ground.

Tower or no, the views from the east peak are superb. USGS Oquossoc, Cupsuptic, and Rangeley quadrangles are useful to have along, as they will help you identify the beautiful circle of mountains and lakes that surrounds you. The water to the immediate north of the mountain is, of course, Aziscoos Lake, and above it lies small Parmachenee Lake. West Kennebago Mountain (Hike 10) is north-northeast. The Richardson Ponds and Upper and Lower Richardson lakes are to the immediate east.

Beyond them lie the broad expanses of Mooselookmeguntic and Rangeley lakes, with Saddleback behind (Hike 11). From south to east, the Appalachian Trail runs from Old Speck over Baldpate, Old Blue (Hike 6), and Elephant mountains (Hike 47). The long flank of Elephant nearly hides Tumbledown (Hike 2), barely in sight. To its left are Little Jackson (Hike 3), Big Jackson, and Blueberry mountains. Southwest, past Umbazookus Lake, the Presidential Range rises in New Hampshire. Also in New Hampshire, Magalloway Mountain rises to the northwest.

To descend, carefully retrace your steps down the mountain. Use caution not to lose the trail in blowdown.

10

West Kennebago Mountain

Total distance (round trip): 4.5 miles
Hiking time: 3 hours
Vertical rise: 1,800 feet
Map: USGS 15' Cupsuptic

West Kennebago Mountain couldn't be better situated if it tried. The long ridge rises far back in paper company woodlands a good ten miles from the blandishments of civilization (such as the nearest tarred road). Only ten miles from Canada on its north side, the mountain is one of the eastern links in a long horseshoe-shaped range of hills that runs down from Seven Ponds, through Upper and Lower Cupsuptic, and back up to Oxbow. The views are splendid.

To reach the mountain, go first to the Maine Forest Service station at Toothaker Brook, 4.5 miles north and west of Oquossoc on ME 16. A good local map is available free here; it will help you navigate the timber road. Fire permits (if you're camping in an undesignated area) can be obtained here, too.

Proceed west from the station for .3 mile on ME 16. Turn right onto a gravel tote road. This route (Old Cupsuptic Tote Road) proceeds through former Brown Company timberlands for 2 miles, where you turn right. Continue on this right-hand gravel road for just over 2 miles, where you again bear right onto a wide, well-groomed gravel road that runs toward the northeast. Proceed eastward 7 miles, watching on the left of the

road for a small sign that indicates the trail to the firetower. Park your car well off the road—this is a route for heavy logging trucks.

The trail follows a rough jeep road toward the warden's camp, with both sides of the road grown shoulder high with wild raspberry bushes. Berry picking and munching will inevitably slow you down a bit in this section, if the season is right (usually late July). Several turnouts are passed on the left as you ascend beyond .2 mile; turn gradually to the west-northwest and climb rapidly.

Just under .5 mile, you pass a final turnout (beyond which the road is impassable even for four-wheel-drive vehicles) and make a dog's leg to the left, climbing steeply through young cherry trees. You shortly turn hard west again, ascend the first of two ridges, slab the second ridge past a large granite outcrop, and then traverse to the west through fragrant, young balsam. At about the 1-mile point, you reach a brook. Continue over several small brooks as you climb south and southwest and, following the signs, turn west again up a steep, pastured slope to the warden's camp at approximately the 1.5 mile point. There are excellent views south from the camp yard.

In the next .3 mile, the trail proceeds northwest above the warden's place, turns west soon, and rises through more fine stands of mature balsam to the height of land. The route then swings quickly over to the south as you ridge-walk on an easy, grassy path just below timberline. The old telephone lines from the warden's camp to the tower run through the trees on your left. A cutover strip is passed with good views to the east and west, and the firetower is reached after 2¼ miles of walking from the trailhead.

The tower on West Kennebago is usually open to visitors when the warden is present. The views of uninterrupted wilderness and mountain terrain are first-class. Kennebago Lake is below to the east, while Cupsuptic Lake is nearly due south. Lincoln Pond (below Big Buck Mountain) and Aziscoos Lake are to the southwest. The ridge that forms West Kennebago runs to the north, and beyond it are Twin Mountains, Snow Mountain, and the range known as the Kennebago Divide. Burnt Mountain is the summit below to the southwest, while Cupsuptic Mountain rises to the west, opposite. If ever there were a series of views almost painfully beautiful, certainly these from West Kennebago are such.

When Ken Spalding was fire warden, my family had the pleasure of taking a winter trip with him to his cabin. We hiked on snowshoes and carried back-

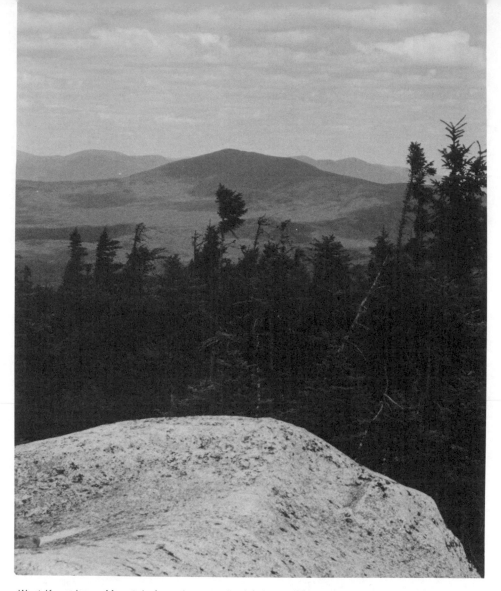

West Kennebago Mountain from the summit of Aziscoos Mountain

packs as far as the cabin, where we spent the night. In spite of January weather, the cabin was cozy with a fire in the woodstove that we kept roaring. The next day, we snowshoed to the tower and spent most of the day admiring the snowy winterscape from the tower and the cutover area.

When last on the mountain, I had the chance to see several spruce grouse in the brush around the summit, and I have seen a female marsh hawk soaring above the road below, searching for prey. As I said, it's a remote area.

Once you've savored that remoteness, return to your car by the route you came up.

11

Saddleback Mountain

Total distance (round trip): 10.2 miles
Hiking time: 7½ hours
Vertical rise: 2,900 feet
Maps: USGS 7.5' Saddleback Mountain, Redington; USGS 15'
  Rangeley, Phillips; MATC Map 6 (1988)

Saddleback, from a distance, lies like a sleeping giant southwest of Rangeley. It is a great mountain with several open summits, two of which are over 4,000 feet high. Its main summit is barren and exposed so that windy, wet weather on the mountain can be hazardous. Even on warm, calm days in the valley, the upper reaches of Saddleback above Eddy Pond can prove cold and treacherous.

Although a shorter trail reaches the summit from the ski area on the northwest side of the mountain, a far more interesting, if more lengthy, approach can be made via the Appalachian Trail (AT). This route affords a full day's hiking in attractive backcountry woodlands well populated with deer, moose, bear, and fox. I consider it, along with the circuit over Bigelow and the long hike onto Mount Abraham, one of the best extended day walks in western Maine.

A substantial portion of the AT has in recent years been relocated southeast of Rangeley. The AT now leaves the north side of ME 4 9.5 miles east of the center of Rangeley and about 2.5 miles west of Madrid. A gravel turnout provides room to leave your car here at an S curve in the road.

From the road, you walk through a dense grove of fir and down a rib to the east. In minutes, you reach and cross the Sandy River, continuing uphill eastward over a low ridge recently logged. The trail runs through a boggy area and shortly crosses a gravel tote road, running more to the north-northeast. You next walk on nearly level ground through an area marked by blowdown, past a cutover on your right, and then ascend north-northwest amidst attractive, dense red spruce and balsam. These woods are rife with spruce grouse pecking about the underbrush, and you are very likely to see some.

Passing a couple of open spots on the left where you may glimpse the Sandy River Ponds, the trail crests a hummock and crosses a boggy area. You cross two barely discernible tote roads at right angles in a few moments and arrive, by a stream, at the junction of the old Sandy River Ponds link trail. On a recent trip along here, I nearly stepped on a large, male fox who burst from the brush just in front of me and bounded ahead, his thick winter brush sailing along behind him.

You now walk around to the east-northeast, with a high steep ridge to

Rock Pond

Midway Pond

Saddleback Mtn

Eddy Pond

Ledge Pond

Moose and Deer Pond

Saddleback

Ethel Pond

Saddleback Pond

Saddleback Pond

Little Saddleback Pond

The Caves

Sandy River Ponds Link Trail

River

Ponds

Stream

Perry Mtn

SANDY RIVER PLANTATION

MADRID

The Horn

N

0   0.5   1.0 mile

P

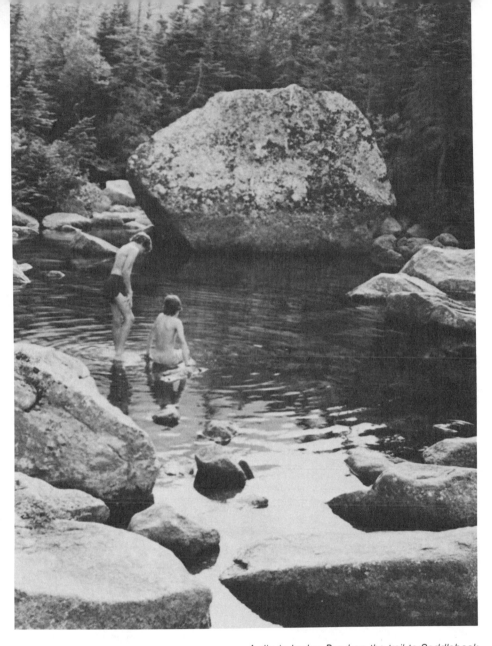

A dip in Ledge Pond on the trail to Saddleback

your left, and arrive at Piazza Rock Lean-to. A short side trail leads left to Piazza Rock, a great, hanging granitic outcrop. From the lean-to, 1.5 miles from the road, you continue northeast-ward, shortly passing another side trail to some rock slabs known as the Caves. The trail runs eastward and south of the ridge or bluff, then begins to climb the ridge steeply, thence dropping down to

Ethel Pond, where you walk the length of the pond's boggy, rutted west shore. Boulders and frequent blowdown mark the trail above the pond.

Past the pond, you climb easily toward the north and northwest over a moss-carpeted way among stands of balsam. Turning northeast, you cross Saddleback Stream, rise gradually through a series of boggy areas, pass a falls on your left, and soon come in sight of Mud Pond, also on your left. The going here is generally mucky, even in dry weather. You're likely to see moose tracks in the wet ground.

Swinging to the northwest on easy grades, you pass through stands of red spruce on a mossy, rock-strewn path, and arrive at a lookout above Eddy Pond. The southwest ledges of Saddleback are visible to the northeast. The steep climbing lies ahead. Walking to the east-northeast, you skirt the south end of Eddy pond and pass through a mucky area grown up with bunchberries and young balsam. A grassy tote road is crossed, then the trail bears left and follows the east shore of the pond for a short distance. It is wet through here also, and you'll cross several small brooks. Don't be led astray by snowmobile trails. Stay on the white-blazed AT.

At 3.2 miles from the road, you bear to the northeast and cross another gravel tote road, re-entering the woods immediately. You climb steadily here on a rooty, rocky path, ascending generally northeast and east toward the ledges. The trail runs through gradually thinning scrub with occasional views to the northwest and west.

Four miles from your car, you breach the timberline and, climbing steeply, emerge on the ledges. The walk is now completely in the open with the main summit of Saddleback visible ahead. Views to the east to Mount Abraham (Hike 12) open up here. You'll shortly pass a link trail on your left that runs to the ski slopes (in bad weather, descending to the ski area is the fastest, safest way off the exposed ridge). Dropping momentarily into a slump, the trail climbs briskly up the main 4,116-foot summit of Saddleback at just over 5 miles from your starting point.

It is worth taking along the four USGS quadrangles that cover this area, so fine are the views and so numerous the lakes and mountains seen from here (USGS 15′ maps: Rangeley, Stratton, Phillips, and Kennebago Lake). Most striking is the long ridge of Mount Abraham to the east. The Horn, Saddleback Junior, and Poplar Ridge form the subsidiary summits immediately to the northeast.

Saddleback is a huge mound of Devonian granodiorite, similar to granite but slightly darker. It was formed underground, like an enormous blister, where it gradually cooled and hardened. Since then, millions of years of erosion have worn down its rock covering and exposed the granodiorite underneath. The flashy flecks are muscovite mica, which make Saddleback a sparkling gem on a sunny day.

Remember to carry extra clothing (waterproof) and food when making this ascent. Head down if high winds, rain, and clouds make finding the route difficult above treeline. Map 6 in the 1988 *Guide to the Appalachian Trail in Maine* is a useful companion on this walk.

12

Mount Abraham

Total distance (round trip): 8¹/₄ miles
Hiking time: 6 hours
Vertical rise: 3,050 feet
Maps: USGS 7.5' Mount Abraham; USGS 15' Kingfield,
  Phillips

There is no mistaking Abraham. The mountain's bulldog brow peers boldly southeast over Kingfield, while its several summits run imposingly northwest toward Sugarloaf. No foothill, Abraham towers over 4,000 feet above sea level at its highest, and subsidiary peaks are just under 4,000 feet. The barren and exposed rock field leading to the main summit might remind you of Mount Washington's cone. Because Abraham lies in timberlands well back from the road, you'll experience a variety of walking/climbing terrain before reaching the top.

Entry to the mountain is gained via Kingfield. Traveling on ME 16-27, go north of the town center less than .3 mile, and turn on the paved road next to the Jordan Lumber Company sign. Follow this road, which is unpaved after 2.8 miles, to the west and northwest. Continue straight ahead when the road divides at 3.5 miles. As of this writing, I've found the road to be roughest in this section. It shortly smoothes out (but don't expect the Hollywood Freeway), and by proceeding carefully you should be able to drive to the 6-mile-point, turning left and parking by Rapid Stream. A

plank bridge that formerly crossed the stream here has been washed out. The stream must now be crossed over a series of rocks in the stream bed. Use caution; a pole or hiking staff may make your crossing easier.

The foot trail runs west over the stream, then quickly bears right along the route of the logging road. On a slight rise, you walk west and northwest along the road, reaching a T-shaped junction at .5 mile. The trail continues west into the woods here (white sign). Moose range widely through the next 2 miles of trail.

Once in the woods, you climb briefly west-southwest for 50 yards on a boggy, grassy road, cross Norton Brook, and rise easily through a corridor of thinned-out oaks to the northwest. Turning sharply to the north, you slab an abrupt ridge to the right, and then turn west again on higher ground. The trail winds through a cutover area of young oak, and continues north-northwest on a grassy road into denser woods.

Climbing very slightly, you soon pass a second cutover area and follow the trail through a mucky section that is usually a problem even in dry weather. As you enter a third cutover, the trail bears more toward the west again. The trail drops into a slight depression as you cross one of the feeder brooks of Rapid Stream. A short rise and descent brings you to another brook. Climbing more rapidly now, the path moves again to the west and northwest. It crosses three logging roads that run at right angles to the northeast, spans another attractive brook with falls, and soon arrives at the old warden's cabin. The cabin has been used as a hostel of sorts in recent years and is not usually locked.

The ascent from the cabin contrasts with your travel thus far. The trail will climb nearly 2,000 feet in the next 1.5 miles. Your route lies southwest of the cabin. Shortly it turns more westerly, passing through two steep S turns as it ascends the central cone. You pass up through dwarf spruce, young balsam, and clusters of bright red bunchberries and bear around to the southwest again, reaching the boulder-strewn

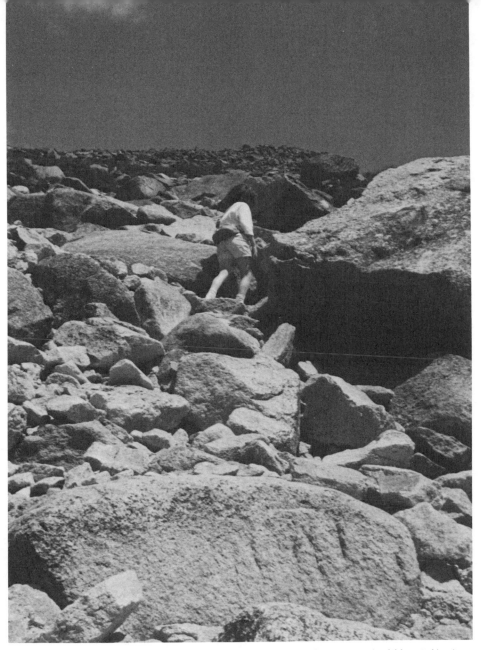

Scree summit of Mount Abraham

home stretch below the summits.

The views are as good here as anywhere in the Maine mountains. The overlook takes in the second-highest peak in Maine, Sugarloaf (Hike 48), directly to the north. To its left looms the high shoulder of Spaulding Mountain. Burnt Hill, Owl's Head, and Black Nubble form a ring to the northeast. In good weather, you can see beyond Sugarloaf to the great east-west ridge of Bigelow Mountain (Hike 13).

The trail continues .5 mile to the summit over the rock field. Follow the cairns and downed telephone line to the old tower site. Because this is an extremely exposed position, caution is necessary in wet, cold weather. At the summit, a cave has been hollowed out of the scree. In bad weather, you can find shelter inside.

One weekend in early May, a friend and I hiked up Mount Abraham and spent the night in the cave at the summit. It is no glamorous accommodation, but someone had placed planks inside which kept us off the ice underneath. While lying in our sleeping bags, we cooked our "Macaroni Massacree" by candlelight on a mountain stove between us and spent a pleasant evening talking. The next day, we had all day to explore the four miles of Abraham's summit before climbing back down. The summit is a long ridge of scree, broken rock rubble that was once part of the mountain's bedrock. Abraham, like its neighbor Bigelow, is metamorphic sandstone, schist, and slate, but its entire ridge appears greenish because the rocks are covered with lichen.

Note: The lower section of this trail has recently been limbed out and is generally easy to follow. The steep, upper section is frequently blocked by blowdown, and extra time should be allowed for getting through.

Follow the same route on the descent.

Bigelow, The Forks, To Jackman

INTRODUCTION

Between ME 27 and US 201 in northwest Maine, a large area untracked by tarred roads offers some of the state's best hiking and adventuring. Its wildness and remoteness make it one of my favorite areas for hiking. Mostly in Somerset County, this is the westernmost region of Maine above Rangeley. The area is remote enough to assure sightings of moose, deer, and possibly black bear. Feathered wildlife lives here in abundance, including the rare spruce grouse, a protected cousin of the ruffed grouse, with its characteristic red eye. Its nickname "fool's hen" is derived from its habit of standing on a branch or on the ground while you walk up to it. The protective law also results from this trait.

At the southwestern end of this section, the many peaks of Bigelow rise in challenge from the Carrabassett River Valley near ME 27, a scenic river drive. The Bigelow Range begins in Stratton and includes Cranberry Peak (Hike 15), the Horns, West, and Avery peaks (Hike 13), and Little Bigelow (Hike 14). This range overlooks Flagstaff Lake to the east, whose history is described in Hike 15. Farther north on ME 27, Cathedral Pines Campground offers camping on the shore of Flagstaff Lake. Still farther north, past Snow Mountain (Hike 16), lies the beautiful Chain of Ponds, which Benedict Arnold's army did not consider all that beautiful when trying to negotiate them by bateau in winter (for a description of Arnold's march, see Hike 16). There are some private campgrounds at Chain of Ponds.

The Bigelow area also offers lots of cross-country skiing on groomed trails in the Carrabassett Valley, and Sugarloaf provides downhill skiing on Maine's second highest mountain, as well as cross-country trails. The Sugarloaf gondola, which carries skiers to the top of the mountain, operates in all seasons. It makes an excellent ride during fall foliage season, and it offers an easy alternative way to climb Sugarloaf (Hike 48). Using the Mount Abraham hike (Hike 12) and the Appalachian Trail (AT), you could plan a large traverse using the Sugarloaf gondola, hiking the AT to Mount Abraham, and hiking down to Kingfield. With some imagination, the gondola could be part of an adventure in any season.

The Forks is named for its location at the fork of the Kennebec and Dead rivers north of Wyman Dam on US 201. The AT passes through this area over Moxie Bald (Hike 19) and Pleasant Pond (Hike 17) mountains, in the heart of white-water canoeing and rafting country. Along US 201 you'll see the headquarters of the different rafting companies, which usually require reservations. Raft trips are guided regularly through the wild and deep Kennebec Gorge, the exciting Dead River, and the challenging West Branch of the Penobscot. For white-water canoeing, inquire at Ed Webb's store on US 201 in The Forks. At Webb's, you can camp, rent canoes or kayaks, and hire transportation to canoe the lower Dead River, famous for its nearly continuous white-water Class III and IV rapids, dropping over four hundred vertical feet in fifteen miles. As campgrounds are small and limited in this area, the Maine Forest Service (MFS) wilderness campsites will be useful.

Jackman, at the northern end of US 201, grew up as the last railroad station before the Quebec border. Now the town offers a variety of outdoor pursuits: fishing, guided or unguided; deer, moose, and bear hunting; snowmobiling and cross-country skiing; lots of four-wheel driving on a vast network of logging roads; and some hiking and canoeing. Jackman's famous canoe trip, the "Bow Trip," is a three- to four-day flatwater paddling trip through a circuit of lakes with very little portage. From the Bow Trip, you can climb Sally Mountain (Hike 21) and make some climbs that have otherwise difficult access.

There are numerous camps and cabins for rent but no state parks in the Jackman area, so don't go there without your Delorme *Maine Atlas and Gazetteer* for locating MFS wilderness campsites.

13

Bigelow Mountain Loop

Total distance (around loop): 11 miles
Hiking time: 7½ hours
Vertical rise: 2,850 feet
Maps: USGS 15' Stratton; MATC Map 5 (1988)

Bigelow must rank as one of Maine's greatest mountains for its size, ruggedness, beauty, and challenge to the hiker. A wild and unspoiled mountain (it was saved from heavy resort development by concerted citizen opposition), Bigelow constitutes a range of six major summits nearly nine miles in length, running west to east. The range is over twelve miles in length if one includes connected Little Bigelow Mountain with its three lower summits. Views over beautiful Flagstaff Lake north to Canada, and to the many mountains that lie to the south and west, make Bigelow one of the two or three best vantage points in Maine.

One of the less-traveled routes to Horns Pond and to the Horns, West, and Avery peaks runs over the rerouted Horns Trail from Stratton Brook Pond. The trail is located by heading in on a dirt road that runs east from ME 16–ME27, about 3.3 miles north and west of the Sugarloaf Mountain Road and 4.5 miles east of Stratton. Though rough in places, the road can be driven the 2.3 miles to a small clearing above one of the inlet streams to Stratton Pond. Park off the track here.

From the clearing, walk northeast and north on a gravel road around the bog above Stratton Pond. You shortly reach the junction of the Horns Trail and the Fire Warden's Trail. Keep right here, as the old Horns Trail route is not in use and provides an unreliable approach to the ridge. Follow the Fire Warden's Trail to the right as it runs on a distinct logging road to the northeast through stands of pretty, tall birches and red oak. You soon bear more to the east, cross a seasonal brook, and slab briskly up a ridge.

In minutes you ascend a ledge to the northeast and then walk over a series of low rolling ridges. You level off briefly and then descend through birch and balsam groves to a gully bisected by a small brook. Moving up out of the gully, you continue on a logging road to the northeast, arriving at a trail junction 1.2 miles from the clearing where you parked. (Watch carefully for signs here; they are posted rather high up on the trees and may be missed.)

The new Horns Pond link bears *left* here and runs northwest through an attractive area of second-growth forest, which is at its most colorful in autumn. The blue-blazed trail begins its ascent of a series of ridges to the northwest, ris-

Bigelow seen from Cranberry Peak

ing gradually into stands of balsam, birch, and maple. The trail soon joins another woods road, and you walk more steeply northwest, crossing several brooks. A side trail is passed shortly above the most prominent brook. The trail leads to good views over Sugarloaf and Crocker mountains (Hike 48). Still ascending northwest, you cross several more brooks, and pull abruptly left off the road and over a boggy hummock. The trail follows the south side of a marsh here, and there are open spots where you can see up to the south Horn.

Passing a second outlook to the left where there are further views across to Sugarloaf, you walk northwest again through dense, low balsam and mossy groundcover. The trail rises steadily to a junction with the Appalachian Trail (AT)

4 miles from your starting point. Bear right here, and in a few moments arrive at Horns Pond shelters. The two lean-tos and several tent platforms offer good camping, but the facilities are heavily used in high summer, and finding space may require an early arrival. A trail behind the northernmost of the two shelters leads, in a few yards, to the shore of strikingly beautiful Horns Pond.

From the clearing around the shelters, you head northeast and east on the AT, climbing steadily through balsam and red spruce. The going is often muddy in this section. As you ascend, you'll have occasional views back to Cranberry Peak west of the pond. The northernmost of the two Horns comes into view shortly, and you momentarily pass the connector trail to the left, arriving on the summit of the south Horn. The views here to the east, south, and west are superb. Horns Pond lies like a small mirror in the col to the west. Canada jays, gray-and-white robbers, will land and eat from your hand if you share your lunch with them.

The trail now dips several hundred feet into a depression as it runs eastward through spruce and balsam scrub, and then gradually ascends the ridge again on increasingly steep grades to Bigelow's West Peak. This is the highest summit on the range at 4,150 feet, and

there are spectacular views to the north over the long, thin strip of Flagstaff Lake, northeast toward Katahdin (Hikes 33 and 34), and south and west to Sugarloaf (Hike 48) and Saddleback (Hike 11). West Peak gets the full brunt of the cold Canadian winds, so pack along extra clothing, particularly if you're hiking Bigelow in the autumn.

Once off West Peak, you descend sharply eastward to the Myron H. Avery Lean-to just below Avery Peak. This shelter makes a good place to camp out of the wind. There is a spring nearby. From the lean-to, you climb Avery Peak to the east over steep grades, arriving on the summit in .4 mile. Splendid views to the east are the rule here, especially over the widest section of Flagstaff Lake and Little Bigelow Mountain (Hike 14), immediately below.

To descend, retrace your steps down to the lean-to on Bigelow Col, turning left or south on the Fire Warden's Trail. The route turns more to the southwest shortly, descending steeply over a series of ladders, rock steps, and terraces. You'll lose about 1,500 feet of elevation in about 1.2 miles. The grade slackens abruptly, and you continue southwest, crossing several barely discernible woods roads as you proceed downward through young beech and maple. The trail isn't well marked in this section, but it is easy to follow. Just under 2 miles from Avery Lean-to, you pass the Horns Pond link to the right that you followed on your ascent. Continue *straight on* to the southwest here. The trail meanders in and out of a prominent logging road. Watch carefully for the point where the path abruptly leaves the road and runs more to the southwest. This turn can be missed easily at dusk.

The trail then descends a series of grassy ridges, crosses a brook, and continues southwest in the boggy depression you walked through on your way up. The logging road is regained shortly, and you stay with it to the southwest and to the clearing where you parked.

Much of your walking on this loop lies in sheltered areas. The main ridge, including the Horns, West, and Avery peaks, is dangerously exposed and, as we suggested earlier, tends to collect inclement weather from the northwest. A mild sunny day down on the road will give little warning that high winds and near-zero chill factors may prevail on the peaks. Because this is a long route, fatigue also becomes a consideration as you walk over the summits. You should carry extra clothing, including rain gear, and plenty of food and water. A flashlight may come in handy. If you're climbing in September, October, or November, it'll probably be dark before you reach the road on the final leg of the loop.

14

Little Bigelow

Total distance: 12 miles
Hiking time: 8 hours
Vertical rise: 2,000 feet
Maps: USGS 15' Little Bigelow Mountain; MATC 5 (1988)

Little Bigelow, in Dead River Township, rises from the southeast end of Flagstaff Lake in the wilderness of Somerset County. It is the easternmost of the six peaks in the seventeen-mile-long Bigelow Range. A circuit hike using 6 miles of the Appalachian Trail (AT) across Little Bigelow's ridge, the 1.5-mile Safford Brook Trail descent at the west end of the ridge, and 4.5 miles of dirt road along the shore of Flagstaff Lake (no views of the lake) allows you to explore

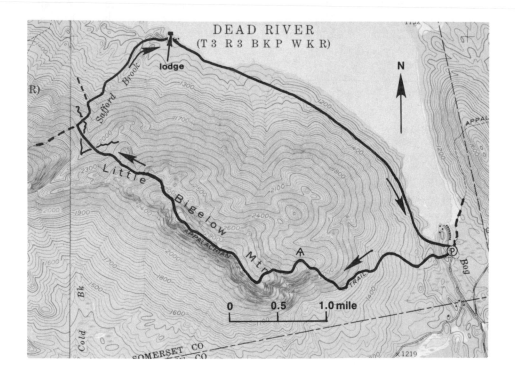

this well-known Maine mountain. To avoid the 4.5 miles of shore road, a car can be spotted where the Safford Brook Trail joins the shore road, a few yards past the driveway to the Bigelow Lodge.

To reach the trail, travel on ME 16 northwest from North Anson or southeast from Kingfield to North New Portland. At the North New Portland Post Office and General Store, leave ME 16 and drive north on Long Falls Dam Road for 17.6 miles and turn left at a group of mailboxes onto Bog Brook Road (dirt). At 18.3 miles take the left fork, and at 18.5 miles, you can see on the left the white paint blazes of the Appalachian Trail where it crosses the road. Back up a few yards and park in the clearing. (If you wish to spot a car at the end of the Safford Brook Trail, continue another 4.5 miles on the road and park in the gravel pit opposite the driveway to Bigelow Lodge.)

Pick up the AT as it crosses the road to the left and rises gently through young hardwoods and some large old cedars. The trail is often muddy where it parallels the brook for the first .5 mile. The trail bears away from the brook and ascends a beech ridge, passing a dry brook on the left. It then ascends more steeply over rocks, passing Indian pipe, Indian cucumber, and very tall rock (sugar) maples.

At 1.9 miles, the trail takes you over boulders and then climbs steeply up through a boulder-filled ravine, almost a grotto. Use caution here, especially if the rocks are wet. Shortly after climbing out of the grotto, you reach the first open ledges and are rewarded with bunchberry, blueberries, and views north over Flagstaff Lake. The ascent is more gradual beyond, following cairns through open ledges with blueberries, sheep laurel, and reindeer lichen, and ducking into thick spruce and fir forests.

On the ground you can find leaves and berries of wintergreen (teaberry) to chew.

At 2.9 miles, you reach little Bigelow's summit (3,040 feet), with views northwest to Avery Peak on Bigelow (Hike 13), over the Carrabassett Valley southwest to Sugarloaf with Crocker Mountain on its right (Hike 48), south to Mount Abraham (Hike 12), and southeast to Stewart Mountain.

Continue walking the ridge northwest toward Bigelow. The trail is rough and passes over a series of knobs on the long crest of Little Bigelow. At 4.2 miles, the trail begins a long gradual descent, winding in and out of ledges — some with views north, others with views south. Wood sorrel, Canada mayflower, wintergreen, and spinulose wood fern grow along the way, as well as starflower, asters, clintonia lily, sarsaparilla, and bunchberry. The descent steepens and is slippery and dangerous when wet. You cross a tributary of Safford Brook and descend through maples and white birch, crossing the brook again on the remains of an old bridge. Shortly, at a huge cedar, two forks of the brook converge into the mainstream of Safford Brook.

At 6 miles, turn right onto the 1.5-mile-long Safford Brook Trail. (The AT turns left uphill to Avery Peak.) The Safford Brook Trail soon crosses the brook on an old bridge and runs onto an old tote road, the old "Dead River Route" that was part of the Appalachian Trail in the 1930s before Flagstaff Lake was formed in 1949. The road descends gradually through beech and maple and runs into a gravel pit. Unless you spotted a car here, turn right and walk the dirt road east 4.5 miles, past the driveway to Bigelow Lodge (locked gate) on your left and back to the trailhead where you parked.

Ascending Little Bigelow's rock grotto

Before returning on the dirt road, you may want to follow the Safford Brook Trail left from the gravel pit to the shore of Flagstaff Lake. Along the shore to the west is a field where a round barn used to stand. Only the stone foundation remains, but the field is still called the "round barn field."

In June 1976 a ten-year battle climaxed between developers who wanted to make Bigelow an "Aspen of the East" and conservation groups led by the Friends of Bigelow, the Maine Appalachian Trail Club, The Natural Resource Council of Maine, and the Appalachian Mountain Club. A petition drive overrode the legislature and forced a referendum vote, which, by a narrow margin, established the Bigelow preserve, a 35,000-acre wilderness protecting the entire Bigelow Range and a buffer zone around the mountain's base. Long-term management of the preserve is yet to be settled, and the threat presented by the Bigelow Lodge still kindles many a debate.

15

Cranberry Peak

Total distance: 6.4 miles
Hiking time: 4½ hours
Vertical rise: 2,100 feet
Maps: USGS 15' Stratton; MATC 5 (1988)

Cranberry Peak is the westernmost peak of the seventeen-mile-long, east-west Bigelow Range, south of Flagstaff Lake. It makes a pleasant half-day hike with rewarding close views of the Horns of Bigelow and a 360-degree panorama of the western Maine mountains.

The most direct trail to Cranberry Peak is the Bigelow Range Trail, which begins at ME 16-ME 27 in Stratton. Coming from the south, drive .2 mile north of Stratton Brook and turn right onto a dirt road. From the north, drive .6 mile south from the junction of ME 27 and ME 16 and turn left. Continue .1 mile to a sandy opening to park.

The trail leaves east on a gravel road following blue blazes .4 mile to a smaller area where it is also possible to park. In this smaller opening, the trail leaves the road to the left, following blue blazes uphill, downhill, and up again to an old lumber road at .7 mile. Turn left onto the old road and ascend more easily, following the blue blazes at any forks.

The woods are a mixture of tall spruce, birch, and hemlock. On the ground are purple wake-robin, clintonia lily, wild sarsaparilla, and Indian cucumber. At 1.5 miles, a spring on the left (last water) is a good place to fill can-

teens. From the spring, the trail climbs steeply through very large white and yellow birch, maples and striped maple, some large ash, asters, Solomon's plume, long beech fern, and spinulose wood fern. At its steepest part, the trail ascends through huge stately red and white pines. These trees used to be the climax forest growth in Maine, giving it the nickname of Pine Tree State. Now most of the pines are gone from logging and fires, and in their place are faster-growing spruce and balsam fir.

A short side trail among the big pines leads left to an overlook with views west to East and West Kennebago mountains (Hike 10). Below is Stratton, where Flagstaff Lake begins at the North and South Branches of the Dead River. Return to the trail, and continue climbing steeply through more openings. At 1.9 miles you pass Arnold's Well on your right, a deep cleft in the ledge, sometimes holding stagnant water at the bottom. Do not drink the water. Benedict Arnold's route in 1775 followed the Dead River, which has since been dammed into Flagstaff Lake. Even though he did not cross the Bigelow Range, Arnold's Well is named after him. Bigelow Mountain and the Bigelow Range are named after Major

Reaching Cranberry Peak

Timothy Bigelow, a member of the Arnold expedition who climbed the mountain to look for Quebec.

From 2.1 to 2.3 miles, step carefully over the Cranberry Ledges, which offer views of Stratton, Flagstaff Lake, and Sugarloaf to the southeast. Up here among the spruce cliffs, gray Canada jays are residents, and hawks soar above and below you. At 2.3 miles, a short side trail leads left to The Cave, an interesting overhanging granite slab. Continue walking through open ledges where sheep laurel and Labrador tea grow and through moist wooded sections dotted with sphagnum moss and Indian-pipe. The final ascent through scrub blueberries, scrub spruce, and birch takes you at 3.2 miles to bare conical Cranberry Peak (elevation 3,213 feet). From here you will turn around and retrace the trail to your car.

From the summit, to the east rise the two Horns of Bigelow. Behind the South Horn, the cap of West Peak is visible, Avery Peak with its tower is further right, and the long loaf of Little Bigelow (Hike 14) sweeps to the right of Avery. Southeast, Sugarloaf (Hike 48) is easy to spot with its ski trails and communications building. To the south and behind Sugarloaf is contiguous Spaulding Mountain. From here look south to Crocker Mountain (also Hike 48) whose south peak is hidden behind the north peak. Southwest is East Kennebago Mountain, with West Kennebago Mountain behind (Hike 10). Northwest rises Snow Mountain (Hike 16), and north over Flagstaff Lake you can see three-peaked Boundary Bald Mountain far on the horizon and the pointed peak of Coburn Mountain (Hike 20) to the north-northeast. East-northeast it is possible to see the Carry Ponds, through which Arnold's army struggled with their 300 bateaux. (For a more complete description of Arnold's trail, see Hike 16, Snow Mountain.)

Cranberry Peak is a good lunch spot. Mountain cranberries grow in the rock crevices, a welcome addition to lunch. If you walk to the next ledge, several

yards further ahead on the trail, you can look down on Cranberry Pond, beyond which the Appalachian Trail comes into the Bigelow Range Trail for the ascent to Horns Pond, the Horns, and Bigelow's summit.

Flagstaff Lake was formed in 1949 when Central Maine Power Company built Long Falls Dam on the Dead River (the West Branch of the Kennebec), so named because many of its twists and turns were dead water. The Dead River Valley was changed from a series of farming communities to a twenty-two-mile-long storage lake. The former villages of Dead River and Flagstaff now lie under the lake, but occasionally, when the lake is drawn down, old bridge abutments, road beds, foundations, and other signs of the old valley settlements are visible proof that humans once lived and worked below the present lake's water level.

16

Snow Mountain

Total distance: 9.5 miles
Hiking time: 6 hours
Vertical rise: 2,200 feet
Maps: USGS 7.5' Chain of Ponds; USGS 15' Chain Lakes

Snow Mountain, in Alder Stream Township northwest of Stratton, offers remote and scenic hiking in the western Maine wilderness near the Quebec border. From the abandoned Maine Forest Service tower on its summit, which is just short of 4,000 feet high, dramatic panoramas extend long distances in all directions.

To find the trail, drive on ME 27 north from the junction with ME 16 in Stratton, paralleling the North Branch of the Dead River above Flagstaff Lake. At 13.5 miles, turn left on a dirt road just south of a gravel pit (first left after town line). At 2.7 miles from ME 27, bear left when the road forks. The road follows Little Alder Stream. Park at the first bridge.

Begin the hike by walking on down the road and crossing a second bridge. At 1.3 miles, take the left fork, immediately cross and recross Little Alder Stream, and ascend sharply through maple and beech, following the old Snow Mountain Road, which is frequented by moose. Stay on the main west-trending gravel road, avoiding any off-shoots. The road is covered by grass in places and so washed out in others that it looks more like a dry brook. The road rises at a steady grade through al-

ders and then through a forest of young maple, beech, and birch.

An unusual number of woodland birds inhabit the woods along this road. You may see flocks of evening grosbeaks and pine siskins, ravens, spruce grouse, and a barred owl or two, as well as more frequently observed birds: many kinds of sparrows and warblers, chickadees, purple finches, and partridge (ruffed grouse). In the muddy road you will also see moose tracks among the fireweed, joe-pye weed, and goldenrod.

At 3.5 miles, you pass a bog on your left and come to a trail that turns left to Snow Mountain Pond, a picturesque "fly-fishing only" pond. Pass this trail and continue 100 yards to the end of the pond, where a small wooden sign marks the fire warden's trail to the right. Leave the road (which ends at a camp on the pond) and turn right (west-northwest) onto the fire warden's trail, which runs north 1.2 miles to the tower.

The trail is lined with meadow rue, alders, and asters in a spruce-birch forest. It climbs higher into wood sorrel, clintonia lily, starflower, spinulose wood fern, broad beech fern, long beech fern, wild sarsaparilla, hobblebush, bunchberry, rosy twisted-stalk, white and pur-

Bigelow from the northwest, over the inlet to Flagstaff Lake

ple asters, and violets.

As you swish through thick bracken fern, the trail levels out and widens through balsam fir and moss. Pieces of old telephone wire remain here and there. About .7 mile from the tower you cross a spring (difficult to see—look for a pipe) padded with lush sphagnum moss, and shortly you scramble up a rock face.

The last .5 mile rises through a balsam forest where lacerating young balsam fir have overgrown the trail. The route is not difficult to follow, but long pants are advisable. A path from Big Island Pond comes in on the left as you climb northeast, shortly reaching the 3,960-foot wooded summit.

Views from the tower are some of the best in Maine. Look southwest to L Pond on the left and Big Island Pond on the right, west into Quebec, and north to the many summits of Indian Stream Mountain, with Arnold Pond behind to

the left and Chain Lakes or Chain of Ponds behind to the right. Beyond Chain of Ponds, you look into Quebec at Lac Megantic. Look east over Little Alder Stream to Bag Pond Mountain and beyond it northeast to massive Kibby Mountain; look southeast to many-peaked Round Mountain and beyond it to Bigelow (Hike 13) rising over Flagstaff Lake; and scan south to Snow Mountain Pond and beyond to Black Mountain.

From the tower, you can see much of the route Benedict Arnold took during his disastrous journey through Maine into Quebec in October and November 1775. He sailed up the Kennebec River with 1,100 men en route to Quebec City, to attack the largest British outpost north of the thirteen colonies. They left the river near The Forks and carried their bateaux west through the Carry Ponds to the Dead River, which in 1949–1950 was dammed into Flagstaff

Lake. The town of Flagstaff grew up at the site where Arnold planted the staff of his American flag. Flagstaff now lies at the lake's bottom. Shortly, above Stratton at Cathedral Pines, torrential rains and freshets flooded Arnold's camp. It was a wintry October, and the starving men boiled their boots and drank the juice, hoping to get nourishment.

Near Snow Mountain, in six inches of snow, Colonel Enos and three companies turned back because of illness and starvation. Those who went on found the Chain of Ponds treacherous, too, from high winds that made the water rough enough to capsize some of the bateaux. Further north, near Coburn Gore on the Quebec border, the men struggled with their bateaux through the Terrible Carrying Place into mire holes, thickets, swamps, ravines, and over precipices. Many men were lost when they floundered up to their armpits in water and ice. The remnants of the army struggled through Lac Megantic, and finally, on November 10, 500 of the original army of 1,100 arrived at Quebec. It took them a month to recuperate before even beginning their unsuccessful attack on Quebec.

Snow Mountain is formed from the oldest rock in Maine, the pre-Cambrian gneiss of the Chain Lakes Massif. This huge massif stretches to the Jackman area and is over 600 million years old.

When you begin your descent, do not miss the point where your trail turns left and the trail from Big Island Pond goes off to the right. Take care descending through the balsam fir undergrowth, as there are slick rocks underfoot.

17

Pleasant Pond Mountain

Total distance: 2.5 miles
Hiking time: 2 hours
Vertical rise: 1,230 feet
Maps: USGS 7.5' The Forks; USGS 15' The Forks; MATC 4
  (1988)

Pleasant Pond Mountain in Caratunk rises over Pleasant Pond just south of The Forks, where the Upper Kennebec and the Dead River join to become the Kennebec River. From the summit you can look down on the pond and see many of the high western Maine mountains. The steep climb will make you thirsty, so carry water.

To get to the trail up the mountain, drive US 201 to Caratunk, 16 miles north of the junction with ME 16 in Bingham. Turn right on the Caratunk Road, drive .3 mile to the post office and general store, and turn left at the intersection. Follow the road along Pleasant Pond Stream to the pond. Fork left at the pond on a road that soon turns to gravel, and drive 1.8 miles to the north end of Pleasant Pond, where you will see an Appalachian Trail (AT) sign. Park here.

From the parking spot, follow the blue-blazed side trail .1 mile to the AT. At the junction, turn right onto the northbound AT. After crossing two dry brooks, begin the steep ascent up gabbro outcroppings in a forest of giant red pine and large cedars. As the trail climbs, views open through the trees to the right (southwest) over Pleasant

Pond. The forest changes to a variety of large hardwoods and spruce, with thin striped maples interspersed. On the ground are wild sarsaparilla, Canada mayflower, starflower, trillium, asters, and spinulose wood fern.

The trail climbs at a steep grade, gaining 1,200 feet in the 1.2 miles to the summit. Parts of the path are severely eroded. The trail climbs through mature hardwoods and softwoods, with various mushrooms living on fallen dead trees. The hardwoods end abruptly as you ascend into conifers: spruce, red pine, white pine, and balsam fir. A steep scramble up eroded bedrock takes you into a beautiful garden of young spruce of perfect form, like miniature Christmas trees. On the ground, their red needles alternate in a checkerboard pattern with patches of green haircap moss.

The trail ascends steeply again through magnificent spruce, crests a rise, and drops down to a trail junction. From here, the old AT heads east downhill to Moxie Pond and Moxie Bald Mountain (Hike 19). Turn right on the new AT that continues .2 mile to the summit of Pleasant Pond Mountain. Two hundred feet up the trail you'll find a small spring on your right, beyond

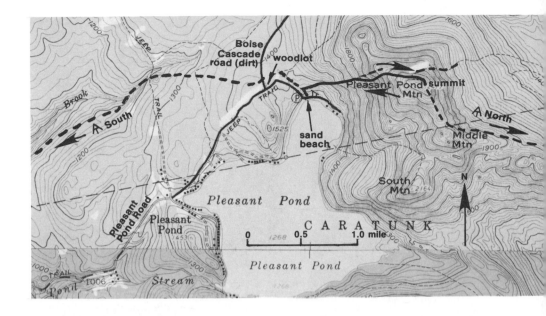

which lie the charred ruins of the fire warden's camp. The trail then rises over the open gabbro summit through dwarfed spruce and sheep laurel, beautiful in July, and ends at the underpinnings of the firetower that used to stand on the 2,480-foot-peak.

Views are perfect in all directions if you walk around the summit. To the northeast, Hedgehog Hill sits like a gumdrop over Moxie Pond, and behind it Big Squaw (Hike 28) rises over Moosehead Lake. Look east over Moxie Pond to Moxie Bald Mountain (Hike 19), and south to the large wooded hulk of Moxie Mountain. Southwest beyond Pleasant Pond are the many peaks of Bigelow (Hike 13), with Sugarloaf (Hike 48) and Mount Abraham (Hike 12) to their southwest. To the northwest is Coburn Mountain (Hike 20).

Return by the same trail, which will be much easier going down. On your return, you will probably want to walk to the lakeshore to see the Pleasant Pond lean-to. If it's especially hot, you can dip in the icy waters of Pleasant Pond at the sandy beach just past the lean-to. The water is always exhilarating, even on the warmest summer days.

At the Kennebec River in Caratunk, you are just east of the Carry Ponds, named for the difficulties Benedict Arnold and his troops had when carrying their 300 bateaux from East to Middle to West Carry ponds and then to the Dead River. Not only was the portage difficult, but the army was near starvation and freezing from the wintry October weather of 1775. The AT partly follows Arnold's trail from the Kennebec River west to Flagstaff Lake.

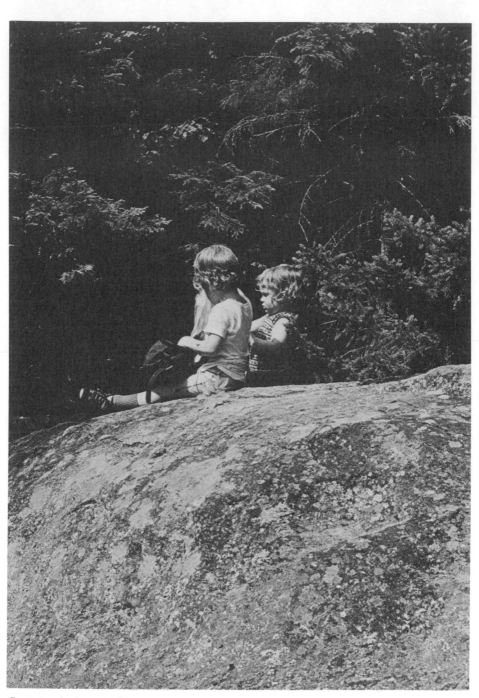

Rest stop for Ian and Skye

18

Moxie Falls

Total distance: 3.5 miles
Hiking time: 2 hours
Vertical rise: 40 feet
Map: USGS 7.5' The Forks; USGS 15' The Forks

Moxie Falls in The Forks rewards hikers with startling beauty for little effort. The eighty-nine-foot falls have been rated the highest in New England, and the setting, a gorge carved through slate, is equally dramatic.

To reach the trail, travel US 201 to The Forks, 48 miles north of Skowhegan and 23.4 miles north of the junction of ME 16 and US 201 in Bingham. At the

bridge over the Kennebec, turn east onto the Moxie Lake Road on the south side of the river. At this turn, there is a picnic area with tables and public facilities. Follow this road 2.7 miles to a parking area with a Moxie Falls sign.

The trail is fairly level, taking you through lovely woods to a boardwalk leading to Moxie Stream, where you will find the introductory upper falls to the

Moxie Falls

right and the dramatic lower falls to the left. The upper falls are a series of step falls coursing through pyramidal slabs of Devonian slate and schist. There is no trail upstream, but you can make your way up the bank.

The boardwalk follows the bank left and downstream to the eighty-nine-foot lower falls. Be careful if you walk out onto the falls! Not even vibram soles will grip wet, water-polished rock. The falls roar down into a gorge walled with schist and rimmed with rock fern on sphagnum moss. Cedars and spruce grow from vertical walls, and more mature cedars surround the rim. The trail skirts about a quarter of the rim, arriving at a beech and birch knoll, the best vantage point for viewing the falls. Some of the older trees are hung with old man's beard lichen. In spring you'll see the white blossoms of Canada mayflower and bunchberry and, in late summer and fall, their red berries. In summer, you can find the tiny yellow blooms of the northern honeysuckle. The only vertical rise is encountered when you retrace the trail to your car.

Winter is my favorite time to visit the falls. Besides the advantages of no people and no bugs, the scene is a fairyland. Most of the trees are evergreen, and the snow is beautiful against the dark spruce and the rusty green of the cedars. The trail I leave with my snowshoes is embroidered with tracks of rabbit, red squirrel, deer, grouse, and an occasional moose. The step falls are invisible under snow-covered ice, but mink tracks leading from hole to hole reveal where ice remains open. The high falls appear frozen at a standstill, but you can hear the rushing of the unseen water underneath. The falls are different every winter: sometimes hung with long tresses of icicles, sometimes frothy and white, sometimes topaz or aquamarine. It is an easy hike on properly maintained showshoes.

19

Moxie Bald Mountain

Total distance: 9.5 miles
Hiking time: 5 hours
Vertical rise: 1,650 feet
Maps: USGS 7.5' Moxie Pond; USGS 15' The Forks, Bingham;
  MATC 4 (1988)

Moxie Bald Mountain, southeast of The Forks, is a four-mile ridge running north-south above Moxie Pond. On road maps, Moxie Bald is often designated simply "Bald Mountain," but because it is near Moxie Mountain and Moxie Pond, general use is gradually accepting the woodsmen's designation, "Moxie Bald." Extended ledges and open crests make it a panoramic climb in good weather to the abandoned Maine Forest Service tower on the summit. The trail also passes through uncut spruce, fir, and hardwoods, using the Appalachian Trail (AT). Water on the trail is not dependable and should be obtained in advance. Moxie Bald is not a good place to be in bad weather. Even on warm summer days it can be cold on the exposed summit. Be prepared.

The road approach begins at The Forks, 48 miles north of Skowhegan and 23.4 miles north of Bingham. Turn right off US 201 on the south side of the Kennebec River at a picnic area, onto the paved road to Moxie Pond and Indian Pond. Drive 5.3 miles, passing the trail to Moxie Falls (Hike 18), to the dam on Moxie Pond. This used to be Lake Moxie Station when the Maine Central

Railroad ran from Bingham to Lake Moxie (now called Moxie Pond). Turn right (south) and follow the lakeshore on a Scott Paper Company road, which used to be the Maine Central Railroad bed. The rutted road makes driving very slow. Partway down the lake, AT blazes come in from the right, and the AT follows the road for a short distance. You can see Moxie Bald rising over the south end of the lake.

At 7.9 miles, a signpost on the left indicates where the AT leaves the road to the east. Park on the right side of the road and begin walking the trail east at the signpost.

The trail begins by crossing Baker Stream, the inlet of Moxie Pond. At times of high water, use a cable crossing just downstream (left). Across the stream, the trail passes through birches and marsh fern to a powerline cut at .3 mile. The cut reveals slate outcroppings and boulders, sheep laurel and blueberries; then the trail reenters woods of tall spruce. Mosses, trailing arbutus, bracken fern, and wintergreen line the sides of the trail, but the spruce are so thick that the ground below has no undergrowth, only spruce duff.

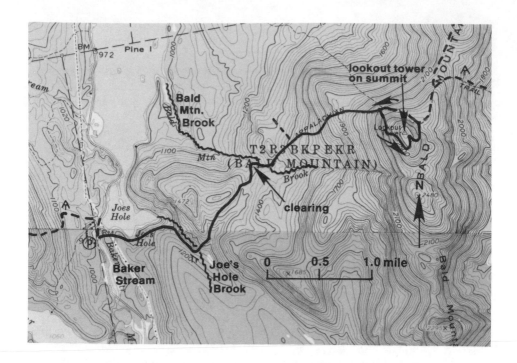

The trail then rises into a beech-maple forest with typical hardwood ground cover: Canada mayflower, starflower, bunchberry, trillium, asters, clintonia lily, violets, wild sarsaparilla, and Indian cucumber. Shrubs are striped maple and hobblebush. Maine woods have two common species of trillium: painted trillium, which has three leaves with three white petals that appear to have been "touched up" with red paint, and purple wakerobin, which has three leaves and three dark red to purple petals and is sometimes called "stinking Benjamin." Both varieties are found in these woods in late May and early June, with purple wakerobin in greater abundance. Moose tracks, too, usually mark the trail.

At 1.1 miles, you pass on your right Joe's Hole lean-to and cross Joe's Hole Brook. Across the brook, the trail continues up an old logging road through mixed growth into spacious, open beech-maple woods, rising gently for the next 1.5 miles.

The woods change to tall black spruce, and at 2.5 miles, you cross an old lumber camp clearing, now filled with raspberries. Cross Bald Mountain Brook and another clearing beyond. From here, the trail begins the ascent of Moxie Bald. Just beyond the brook and clearing, you enter a former campground, where the old fire warden's trail comes in on the left from an abandoned boat landing on Moxie Pond. Follow the white blazes across the campground and to the right, where they enter mature beech, birch, and maple, some of grand size.

Cross a dry brook and ascend more steeply into spruce, with reindeer lichen and mica on the rocky ground. From here, the trail alternates between stands of spruce-fir and stands of hardwoods, as it rises more steeply. Notice how the thin layer of topsoil has eroded to granodiorite bedrock on the trail. This shows the importance of staying on the trail, so that the rest of the woods will not erode.

The trail rises through a garden of sheep laurel and spruce, and levels briefly. Rising steeply again, the trail widens through red spruce, mountain ash, and sheep laurel, until you can see the summit above you on the right. At 3.8 miles, the blue-blazed summit bypass trail turns left and can be used to avoid the open summit in bad weather. It rejoins the AT half a mile later, north of the summit. If the weather is very inclement, however, you should turn around and head back to Joe's Hole and your car.

To continue to the summit, bear right on the AT, which leads in 1/3 mile to the open central (main) summit. This is the steepest part of the hike, through a corridor of young red spruce and bunchberry on a sheer outcrop of granodiorite. Sheep laurel landscapes the bare summit at an elevation of 2,630 feet.

From the tower, a 360-degree panorama surrounds you. Northwest,

Hedgehog Hill is the gumdrop mountain over Moxie Pond. Close by is the north peak of Moxie Bald, which you can reach by an interesting side trip from the AT. Beyond the north peak are Coburn (Hike 20) and Boundary Bald mountains near Jackman. North is Squaw Mountain (Hike 28), and northeast are Big Spencer (Hike 31), White Cap (Hike 27), and in the distance Katahdin (Hikes 33–34). Eastward lies Bald Mountain Pond and behind it, Blue Top. To the south is Moxie Bald's south peak, and southwest is Bigelow (Hike 13) with its two sets of twin peaks. To the west, South, Middle, and Pleasant Pond (Hike 17) mountains rise left to right, with Sugarloaf (Hike 48) and Mount Abraham (Hike 12) in the distance.

To vary your descent, proceed north on the AT. In .3 mile, you will see the blue-blazed summit bypass trail on your left. Use this trail for your return. A spring is located shortly down it.

Before you return, you might want to explore the north peak by continuing north on the AT and taking a side trail to the left. Add 3 miles (round trip) to the distance and 45 minutes to your walking time.

Coburn Mountain

Total distance: 2.4 miles
Hiking time: 1½ hours
Vertical rise: 1,700 feet
Map: USGS 15' Pierce Pond

Coburn Mountain in Upper Enchanted Township south of Jackman is the highest peak in the Jackman area, offering dramatic views from its summit, including Katahdin, Bigelow, and the northern Presidentials of New Hampshire. The mountain was named for Abner and Philander Coburn, early surveyors and extensive landowners of much of western Maine. It is known locally as Enchanted Mountain and is the site of the former Enchanted Mountain Ski Area. A short, steep trail offers quick access to the 3,718-foot summit and tower.

To find the trail, drive on US 201 north 11 miles from The Forks, or 14.8 miles south of the junction of US 201 with ME 6-ME 15 in Jackman Station (2.7 miles south of the Parlin Pond Rest Area). At this point, a wide gravel road turns west from US 201. Your car should have good clearance, and you might need a four-wheel drive. If your car can't negotiate part of this road, you can park and walk. Add the appropriate mileage to the hike. Follow the gravel road 2.1 miles to where it curves right at the site of the former Enchanted Mountain Ski Lodge. Only the concrete foundations of the buildings remain. Park at the old lodge site at the bottom of the swath on Coburn's east face, which used to be the ski slope.

From the lodge site, walk the road north, to the right of the ski slope. The road ascends steeply, crosses a dry brook, and at .4 mile corners left and levels out. From here, the tower is visible at the top of the ridge. At .5 mile, as the road runs into undergrowth, there is a steep, bare, rocky clearing on the right. Leave the road to the left and follow orange flagging from the rocky clearing. From here it is .7 mile to the tower.

The trail enters the woods to the left and, after a few yards, crosses a recent logging cut. Logging slash has obscured the trail here, so use extreme caution. The trail continues on the other side of the logging cut, bearing right and flagged with orange ribbons. Do not follow the blue blazes. The trail is easier to follow after you get through the first few yards of logging slash. It as-

cends through a balsam fir forest with spinulose wood fern, white asters, clintonia lily, wood sorrel, violets, hobblebush, wild sarsaparilla, bunchberry, and purple wake-robin.

At .2 mile you come into the clearing where the fire warden's cabin used to be. The cabin was built in 1908 and burned by the Maine Forest Service (MFS) when the fire tower was discontinued. Only a few traces remain—a bed frame and springs—and the clearing is grown up with six-foot-tall, white-flowered cow parsnip and surrounded by raspberries, a likely lunchground for a bear. (On the opposite side of the clearing, a rocky trail leads 10 yards to a dependable spring, the only water on the trail, and then on for .5 mile to the two small Mountain Ponds.)

Your trail, a phone cable installation route, skirts left at the cabin site and climbs uphill, following remnants of telephone wire through a forest of large balsam fir carpeted with wood-sorrel. The trail curves west and becomes very steep. Although the compacted soil of the trail is easy to follow, balsam branches overgrow the route, making it less than a comfortable ride for a baby or child in a backpack.

As you crest the summit ridge, the trail curves left (west) and levels out for the last spurt to the tower. The bare summit, 1.2 miles from your car, was once used as a helicopter launch pad. When lookouts were discontinued, the MFS tower was toppled over the west side of the mountain. Today a smaller observation tower stands in its place, but the top of the tower is no longer safe.

The views from Coburn's summit rank with the best in Maine: Katahdin, White Cap (Hike 27), Big Spencer (Hike 31), and Bigelow (Hike 13). To the north, behind Bean Brook Mountain, Boundary

Coburn Mountain

Bald Mountain rises eight miles from the Quebec border. Right of Bean Brook Mountain lie Parlin Pond (close) and Long Pond. Northeast over Brassua Lake lies Moosehead Lake with Katahdin (Hikes 33–34) in the distance. Directly east is Big Squaw (Hike 28) overlooking Moosehead. Southeast, Johnson Mountain is the long ridge close by. South-southeast in the distance are Pleasant Pond Mountain (Hike 17) on the left and Moxie Bald Mountain (Hike 19) on the right behind Moxie Pond. South is Pierce Pond with Pierce Pond Mountain to the right. In the south-southwest, the apparent double peak is actually Hurricane and Basin mountains. Far in the distance you can see the entire Bigelow Range (Hikes 13, 14, 15).

Close to the southwest lies Enchanted Pond with Little Enchanted Pond behind and Hardscrabble Mountain beyond on Spencer Lake. Far in the distance, in the same direction, is the northern section of the New Hampshire Presidential Range. West, close by, is Grace Pond. To the northwest, island-filled Attean Pond spreads its entire length below long Sally Mountain (Hike 21). To the right of Attean Pond is Wood Pond, beside which you can see the town of Jackman.

Behind the observation tower, a trail drops east straight down from the summit. This is a good way to complete a circuit back to your car, if you don't mind a steep descent. Head straight down this trail, and in fifteen minutes you will come to the top of the ski slope. From here, walk straight down the ski slope, now grown in with birches, to your car at the lodge site. If you do not want to descend the 1,700 vertical feet in less than 1 mile, you can return by the fire warden's trail that you came on.

I have had two unforgettable experiences on top of Coburn Mountain. One was photographing a family of five partridge—four bold late-summer chicks who let me stand within five feet of them, while their mother tried to tease me away by clucking. The other was in the summer of 1977, as I stood on this mountain with a lump in my throat and watched great clouds of smoke churn up around Katahdin during the Baxter Park Fire.

While you hike back down, you might recall other events that took place not far from Coburn Mountain. Beyond Grace Pond to the west and north of Spencer Lake, on Upper Enchanted Road (also known as the Grace Pond Road), is a place called Hobbstown Depot. It is fifteen miles west of US 201 into the wilderness, and the road is impassable except by four-wheel-drive vehicles. There you can see the remains of a World War II prisoner-of-war camp where 250 German soldiers were imprisoned. One winter a few of them escaped on hand-fashioned showshoes of spruce branches. They were later caught, which is understandable, because there was literally "no place to go" from there.

21

Sally Mountain

Total distance: 6 miles
Hiking time: 4 hours
Vertical rise: 1,000 feet
Map: USGS 15' Attean

Sally Mountain is named for Sally Holden, daughter of Captain Samuel Holden, who was the first settler of the Jackman-Moose River area in 1820. It rises above the town of Jackman between its two principal lakes, Wood Pond and Attean Pond. Its long ridge extends northeast to southwest, and a Maine Forest Service firetower once stood on the southwest summit.

To reach the trailhead, drive north on US 201 to a point south of Jackman Station where ME 6-ME 15 turn east and Attean Road turns west by signs to Attean Lake Resort. Turn left (west) on Attean Road, which soon turns to dirt and is paralleled by a powerline. At 1.4 miles, opposite Central Maine Power pole #31, turn right onto another dirt road and drive 50 yards to a locked gate at the Canadian Pacific Railroad track. Park off the road.

Walk left onto the railroad track, as the first 1.7 miles of the hike follow the track southwest over the Moose River, which connects Wood and Attean ponds, and along the northwest shore of Attean Pond. Cross the Moose River on a railroad bridge, from which you can see on your right the northeast summit of Sally Mountain over Wood Pond. A

powerline parallels the railroad track, which rises gradually from boggy land and cattails through birch and aspen, grasses, bracken fern, and pearly everlasting.

At 1 mile, Attean Pond becomes visible through the trees to the left. This northeast corner of the pond has a large beaver lodge near shore. At 1.7 miles, a few paces beyond power pole #3112, turn right (northwest) and enter the woods on a path. There is no sign, but this is the former fire warden's trail, which leads 1.2 miles to the southwest summit.

The trail is flat, low, and damp, as it runs through dense small birch, balsam fir, and maples. One hundred yards up the trail, cross a small, springfed brook from which the fire warden used to pipe water. Pieces of pipe run along the trail as far as the old cabin site, which is now obscured by underbrush. The trail ascends gently into larger trees, with purple wake-robin, Canada mayflower, starflower, clintonia lily, and wild sarsaparilla on the ground. The trees are predominantly large white birch, striped maple, and several very large aspens.

After .3 mile, the trail steepens. The 1,000-foot vertical rise of this hike is nearly all gained in the last mile to the summit. Various flowers and ferns grow on the steep bank: asters, violets, partridgeberry, white baneberry (doll's eye), Solomon's plume, northern honeysuckle, New York fern, sensitive fern, long beech fern, and large circlets of interrupted fern. After you pass a large balancing boulder on the left, the trail steepens considerably. Here especially you can see some large specimens of Solomon's plume, also called false Solomon's seal and false spikenard. The single stem of one to two feet has alternating oval pointed leaves and frothy white flowers on the end in spring,

which become mottled pink berries in late summer and ruby red in fall.

The trail climbs between massive granite outcroppings up onto open ledges looking southeast over island-dotted Attean Pond. To the east you can see where the two lakes join, and a cut through the trees shows where the railroad skirts the shore of Attean Pond. The last .2 mile crosses open ledges through sheep laurel, lowbush blueberries, and reindeer lichen. Several mountain ash trees have white flowers in summer and red-orange berries in late summer and fall. The trail curves southwest following cairns to the underpin-

View from Sally Mountain summit of Attean Pond, with Coburn Mountain in the background

nings of the former firetower, where the 360-degree panorama sweeps many peaks of northwestern Maine and Quebec and looks down on the lakes of the Jackman area.

To the north, Mud Pond lies to the right of Burnt Jacket Mountain, and behind them part of Little Big Wood Pond is visible. Look north-northeast over Wood Pond to Jackman with Boundary Bald Mountain behind. To the northeast is the northeast summit of Sally Mountain, and below it to the right are the twin Gothic spires of Saint Anthony's Church, Main Street, Jackman. East-northeast beyond Long Pond, Mount Kineo (Hike 29) rises in the distance. East, close by, unnamed hills fill the view, and southeast, Catheart Mountain rises over Attean Pond, with Coburn Mountain (Hike 20) behind it to the right. South beyond Bog Pond runs the

Moose River, and beyond are two peaks of equal elevation, Hardscrabble (left) and Hardwood (right) mountains. Southwest close by is Attean Mountain, and behind to its left are Number Five Mountain on the left with a tower, and Number Six Mountain on the right. To the west behind an unnamed hill are Holeb Pond and Birch Island, behind which are the mountains of Quebec. Sally Mountain is in view for most of the famous "Bow Trip," a canoe circuit of the Moose River—Attean Pond, carry to Holeb Pond, Holeb Stream, and the long Moose River return to Attean Pond.

Your return is by way of the same trail. Throughout the hike, you can hear loons calling on the lakes. They are an endangered species in some places but flourish in these ponds. Even at the summit, their cries are clear, a reminder that you are in wilderness.

Monson to Moosehead

INTRODUCTION

Moosehead Lake, the largest lake east of the Mississippi within one state, lies partly in Somerset County but mainly in Piscataquis County in north-central Maine. It is surrounded by many other lakes of all sizes. Greenville is the town at the southern end of Moosehead, and Monson is about fifteen miles south of it on ME 6 and 15. This section also includes three hikes to the east, near Katahdin Iron Works off ME 11.

Monson, the slate capital of the northeast, has several operating slate quarries, although slate is in less demand these days due to competition from other building materials. Monson is also the first opportunity for southbound Appalachian Trail (AT) hikers to buy food, receive mail, and find amenities of civilization after hiking the "Hundred Mile Wilderness" from Baxter State Park to Monson.

Hikes 22–27 are located in the "Hundred Mile Wilderness." Hikes 25–27 can be reached by traveling to Katahdin Iron Works off ME 11 north of Brownville Junction (see Hike 25 for directions and a description of the iron works). The Gulf Hagas hike (Hike 26) takes you through The Hermitage, a virgin stand of huge white pine protected by The Nature Conservancy, worth seeing even if you don't take the hike.

Accommodations in the Monson area are few. The Maine Forest Service (MFS) Little Wilson Stream Campsite is the only place to camp. Shaw's Boarding Home is a friendly bed and breakfast for hikers. If you stay here, you'll meet the Shaws and some AT hikers, many on their way from Maine to Georgia or vice versa. The only state park in the area, Peaks-Kenny near Dover-Foxcraft, is for day-use only.

Katahdin Iron Works has a large number of campsites along the West Branch of the Pleasant River, White Brook, and other locations here and there in the wilderness.

The Moosehead Lake area has numerous private accommodations, including camping. Your Delorme atlas will show you MFS wilderness campsites in the area. Lily Bay State Park on the eastern side of the lake offers overnight camping, as does Brassua Lake Campground west of Moosehead on ME 6 and 15.

This country is rich in history: the Indian-guided travels of Henry David Thoreau, the log-driving years, the prisoner of war camps hidden here and there in the wilderness (see various hikes for descriptions). It is also rich in wildlife and other natural wonders. You could spend a lot of time getting to know this country.

Big Wilson Cliffs and Little Wilson Falls

Total distance: 3. 5 miles
Hiking time: 2 hours
Vertical rise: 800 feet
Maps: USGS 15' Sebec Lake; MATC 3 (1988)

This hike in the area southeast of Moosehead uses the Appalachian Trail (AT) part of the way. You make an easy tour of slate cliffs for views and finally reach a dramatic set of slate falls. The only water available on this hike is surface water, so you should begin with a full canteen.

To reach the trailhead, drive .5 mile northwest from downtown Monson on ME 6-ME 15, and turn right onto the Elliottsville Road. Drive 7.7 miles almost to Big Wilson Stream; just before you reach the bridge, turn left onto a woods road and drive .7 mile to the Maine Forest Service-maintained Little Wilson Campsite. The hike begins here at the site of a washed-out bridge over Little Wilson Stream. Pick your way across slate falls to the opposite bank of the stream. Look for violets and other surprises growing from cracks in the slate.

The author and her daughter view Little Wilson Stream

After crossing, turn left on a gravel road. After .1 mile, you pass on your right a blue-blazed side trail that runs (northeast) into the woods toward Jim Whyte's Lookout and Big Wilson Cliffs. This trail used to be the AT, but the latter has been rerouted in the aftermath of logging operations. With obliteration of this old trail, the way to Jim Whyte's Lookout is lost along with the first trail to Big Wilson Cliffs.

Continue walking the gravel road approximately 1 mile, rising steadily past slash from logging operations. At 1 mile, the road levels and begins to descend slightly. You will meet the current AT (white blazes) when the road reaches a gravel pit on your right. Directly across from the gravel pit, the AT turns left (sign "AT South"). You will follow the AT South to Little Wilson Falls after you have returned from Big Wilson Cliffs. But first, keep walking up the road, following the white blazes of the AT North for 100 yards, until the white blazes turn right, leaving the road and leading you uphill through the woods. The trail shortly levels and begins to take you east across an open slate cliff. Borestone Mountain (Hike 23) is always ahead of you. Follow the trail over the slate ridge as long as it runs east toward Borestone Mountain. After .5 mile on this ridge, the AT turns north and away from the slate ridge. This is the turn-around point. The ridge runs another .5 mile to Big Wilson Cliffs, but skidders have wrecked the area and left it nearly impassable.

The cliffs here lie in an east-west direction, an unusual orientation for Maine. Because of the direction of bedrock folding in Maine, most ridges run from north to south or northeast to southwest. The gigantic upheaval of bedrock that forms these cliffs forced local drainage patterns to change direction in order to skirt the land mass. This abrupt change in direction and bedrock

hardness caused the uneven topography and the numerous rapids and falls in Big Wilson and Little Wilson streams.

From the cliffs, retrace your steps on the AT back to the gravel road. At the road, follow the AT 100 yards to its turn-off south (right). From here it is .5 mile to Little Wilson Falls. The trail passes a small pond with a beaver dam.

Soon the trail arrives at Little Wilson Stream, where step falls pitch over slate slabs. Pin cherry overhangs the top of the falls, covered with white blossoms in spring. Beside the stream is a natural garden of Jack-in-the-pulpits, which bloom in late May.

Follow the white blazes across the stream. The trail parallels the left bank of the stream, passing more series of falls and pools, and arrives in .3 mile at the top of spectacular, sixty-foot Little Wilson Falls. Massive slate walls enclose the falls, supporting the growth of ferns, mosses, and grasses. This is an excellent place for a picnic, a shower in the falls, or a swim in the pool below.

From the falls, return to the Little Wilson Stream crossing. From here, you can retrace your steps on the AT back to the gravel road, turn right, and walk back down the road to your car. But if you would prefer to return to your car a different way, you can follow Little Wilson Stream back down to the campsite where you parked. The distance is 1 mile, but the going is slow since the rough fishermen's trail crisscrosses the stream from bank to bank. In warm weather, it's fun to walk in the stream, avoiding the deep pools (unless you feel like taking a dip). There is also a large pool in the stream at the campsite for cooling off after a hot hike. Either return takes about 45 minutes.

For two more hikes in the area, see Hike 23, Borestone Mountain, and Hike 24, Barren Mountain.

23

Borestone Mountain

Total distance: 4 miles
Hiking time: 3½ hours
Vertical rise: 1150 feet
Maps: USGS 15' Sebec Lake; MATC 3 (1988)

Like a sparkling gem in the Hundred Mile Wilderness area of the Appalachian Trail, Borestone Mountain offers astounding views and an education in nature with a hike of relatively moderate effort. Until the 1970s, Borestone was private property, but a generous gift from R. T. Moore and his heirs has resulted in a well-kept road, trail, and nature center open to the public and managed by the National Audubon Society as a sanctuary since 1984. In 1985, the north side of the mountain was donated by Dr. John H. Lewis.

The nature center, halfway up the mountain, is operated from June 1 through October 31, when a fee of $1.50 for adults and $1.00 for students is charged for using the trail. At other times of the year, the hike is gated off but can be hiked without benefit of the nature center. The only water on this hike is surface water, so you should begin with a full canteen. The forest of Borestone Mountain, uncut for a century, is mixed hardwoods and softwoods—beech and birch at the bottom grading into spruce and fir towards the top. You'll see some huge "old timers" on this hike.

Borestone is located in the Monson area near Hike 22, "Big Wilson Cliffs

and Little Wilson Falls," and Hike 24, "Barren Mountain." To find the trailhead, drive ME 6-ME 15 north from the center of Monson for .5 mile, and turn right (northeast) onto the Elliotsville Road. Continue 7.8 miles to Big Wilson Stream, cross the bridge, turn left, cross the Canadian Pacific Railroad tracks at 8.5 miles, and at 8.6 miles you'll see the trailhead to Borestone Mountain on the right. Park off the road, taking care not to block the gate in case the ranger needs to drive up or down the trail.

The trail follows the auto road, beginning with a gentle rise through mature beech and birch with smaller moosewood (striped maple) trees scattered throughout. The typical hardwood forest floor is open with wild sarsaparilla, trillium (red and white), and numerous ferns. You can walk the road all the way to the nature center or take a few shortcuts following the trail under the telephone wire.

At .6 mile, a side trail leads 200 feet to the right to Little Greenwood Overlook, with a view to the south of Little Greenwood Pond with Greenwood Mountain, 1100-feet high, behind it to the left. At the right time of summer, you'll find blueberries and blackberries on the ledges. The ledges themselves, made of schist, are scraped in parallel grooves trending south toward Little Greenwood Pond. These grooves are glacial striations gouged by debris at the base of a glacier pushing southward a million years ago.

As you continue up the auto road, the woods change to predominantly spruce, fir, and pine, with sheep laurel and bracken fern in sunny spots like garden shrubbery. At 1.3 miles, you'll see the Robert T. Moore Visitor Center on Sunrise Pond. A little time spent studying the exhibits in the nature center will enhance the rest of your trip. You'll learn that hundreds of plants and numerous animals inhabit these slopes, one of which, the peregrine falcon, is a recently reintroduced resident. You can also see a map of the Onawa Pluton and its effect on the geology of the Borestone area.

Sunrise Pond is the first in a series of three ponds, including Midday and Sunset ponds, named according to the time of day the sun shines on them. The trail leaves the road, curves past the nature center, and makes a quarter circle around the pond. Abruptly, it leaves the pond for a steep spurt of .5 mile through mixed woods, then spruce and fir, then over open ledges, to the barren summit. You will need to use your hands to scramble up some of the rocks, and you'll cross two false summits before reaching the 1947-foot summit.

At the top, iron pins remain as evidence of the former firetower erected in 1914. To the north runs the impressive Barren-Chairback Range, traversed by the Appalachian Trail. From north to northeast, the peaks are Barren, Fourth, Third, Columbus, and Chairback mountains (Hikes 24 and 25). Below you, Lake Onawa spreads north and east, nearly bisected by a delta and dotted with tiny islands. Southward lies Big

Greenwood Pond, and west you can see Midday and Sunset ponds, beyond which the land falls precipitously to Big Wilson Stream Valley.

In the nature center, an exhibit on the local geology reveals an interesting story about the formation of Borestone and its surrounding area. Borestone is part of the massive Onawa Pluton, which encompasses the Lake Onawa area. During the Devonian period, between 390 and 345 million years ago, most of Maine's mountains were built by molten magma either shooting up through the crust (volcanoes) or pushing up huge blisters beneath the crust without bursting the crust. The second method results in granitic mountains such as Borestone, which is granodiorite, slightly darker than granite.

The Onawa Pluton was a "blister" of molten magma that welled up under the surrounding crust or "country rock" of sedimentary rock, mostly shale. Heat from the hot liquid granite baked the surrounding shale country rock into very hard and durable slate and schist (the process of metamorphism). The baked slate and schist, resistant to erosion, remain standing as the Barren-Chairback

Climbing Borestone Mountain

Range, Big Wilson Cliffs, and other mountains in the Onawa area; and the liquid magma that cooled and hardened into granodiorite remains as Borestone Mountain and part of Barren Mountain. Granite and granodiorite are less resistant rock. Lake Onawa lies as proof that much of the pluton (the blister) has eroded away.

Why then is Borestone still standing? At the summit you will notice that the rock is striped with white vein quartz, a result of contact metamorphism between the Onawa Pluton and overlying country rock. This durable metamorphic "cap" on Borestone has withstood weathering, glaciation, and erosion, preserving the mountain, while the rest of the pluton eroded away around it.

Your trail down is the same as your trail up. Watch your footing carefully. Hiking down is more dangerous than hiking up.

Barren Mountain

Total distance: 12.2 miles
Hiking time: 8 hours
Vertical rise: 2,260 feet
Maps: USGS 15' Sebec Lake; MATC 3 (1988)

Barren Mountain, the highest and westernmost peak of the Barren-Chairback Range, looms over Elliottsville Plantation north of Monson. Barren is the last peak in the Hundred Mile Wilderness of the Appalachian Trail (AT) from Abol Bridge south to Monson, which is 12 miles north of Guilford and 14 miles south of Greenville on ME 6-ME 15.

To reach the trails you follow on this hike, take ME 6-ME 15 north from the center of Monson for .5 mile, and then turn right (northeast) on the Elliottsville Road. Continue 7.8 miles to Big Wilson Stream, cross the bridge, and turn left. At 8.5 miles, cross the Canadian Pacific Railroad track and pass the Borestone Mountain Trail, and 10.7 miles from Monson you come to Bodfish Farm, a wide flat expanse. Bear left at the next fork (10.8 miles); the gravel lumber road you follow for the final 1 mile crosses private property as it cuts through Long Pond Stream valley and Bodfish Intervale. Park at the next fork.

Begin walking on the right fork over a rotting bridge across Vaughan Stream. Follow the road, which is washed out in several places beyond the bridge, for half a mile to the AT crossing. Turn right, leaving the road, and follow the white-blazed Appalachian Trail. At .6 mile (not long after you leave the road), you cross Long Pond Stream at a ford, normally knee-deep, and follow the east bank. At 1.2 miles (.7 mile from road), you enter Slugundy Gorge and pass Slugundy Falls. Here, Long Pond Stream has cut sharply into slate bedrock forming the gorge.

A steep ascent then leads uphill through wood sorrel, wild sarsaparilla, and rosy twisted-stalk in mature hardwoods. Cross a dry brook and enter younger growth with some very big rock (sugar) maples. On the ground are foamflower and starflower.

At 1.5 miles you come to a trail junction. (To the left .6 mile is Long Pond Stream lean-to.) Turn right (south) and follow the white blazes toward Barren Ledges. The 1-mile ascent to the ledges steepens as you mount the Barren-Chairback Range. Giant rock maples tower over younger maples and beech, with hobblebush and Indian cucumber beneath. At its steepest, the trail climbs water bars, log steps placed to slow erosion. At the higher reaches, spruce begins to predominate, and you come shortly to slate outcroppings.

The trail corners sharply onto more

outcrops, the trees thin, and views open to the north of the Gulf Hagas Mountains. Immediately, the trail curves south and levels out at the crest of a ridge, still heading south. At 2.6 miles, a side trail leads right 250 feet to an overlook of Barren Slide. Views left to right from the slide are south to Lake Onawa with Borestone Mountain (Hike 23) behind, southwest to Bodfish Intervale (the flat floodplain of Long Pond Stream), and close under the slide to Otter Pond. Beyond are Bodfish Farm and Big Wilson Cliffs (Hike 22). West is Big Squaw Mountain (Hike 27).

Shortly beyond the slide, the trail takes you out onto Barren Ledges, which offer dramatic views of Borestone Mountain rising over Lake Onawa. Beyond the ledges, the trail levels and cuts a hairpin curve through bracken fern, bunchberry, clintonia lily, Canada may-

flower, and blueberries, rising gradually for 1 mile. Moose tracks mark the trail through the gently sloping wooded corridor. Then you ascend sharply .5 mile up the granite cone of Barren Peak, and at 4.4 miles reach the tower at the 2,660-foot summit. The entire length of Barren Mountain is a granodiorite hulk rising above a countryside entirely of slate. (For a description of local geology see Hike 23, Borestone Mountain.) The firetower wasn't erected on Barren Mountain until 1951. Until then fires were scouted from the Borestone tower, which was established in 1914.

Views from the barren summit and the tower rank with the best in the state. To the north, beyond Long Pond, the AT eventually crosses Gulf Hagas Mountain, West Peak, and Hay and White Cap mountains. Beyond White Cap (Hike 27), Katahdin is visible on a clear day. To the east, the AT follows Barren Ridge to Cloud Pond (out of sight) and to the rest of the Barren-Chairback Range: Fourth, Third, Columbus, and Chairback (Hike 25) mountains. To the south is Lake Onawa, and behind it, Sebec Lake. Southwest are Borestone and Bodfish Intervale, and west is Big Squaw (Hike 28). To the north are Big and Little Spencer mountains (Hike 31).

From the tower, continue east on wooded Barren Ridge, losing very little elevation, for 1 mile through balsam fir and bunchberry. At 5.4 miles, a blue-blazed side trail leads right .2 mile to Cloud Pond lean-to. Cloud Pond's 2,409-foot elevation is only 250 feet below the summit elevation of Barren Mountain. This lean-to is one of the nicer places to spend the night on Maine's AT. It is in remote wilderness on a peninsula in Cloud Pond, shielded from wind in a grove of trees. Loons call on the pond, and when it mirrors blue sky and white clouds, you understand why it was named Cloud Pond. Or was it because at 2,409 feet, the pond is up among the clouds? If you should plan to spend the night at the lean-to in summer, it may be filled with hikers. In spring and fall you are more likely to be alone.

Return to the white-blazed AT, turn left, and retrace the trail over Barren's peak and ledges, back through Slugundy Gorge to the road you started on.

To end on a dramatic note, instead of returning straight to your car, follow the AT South as it leaves the road to the right (west), and walk .5 mile to Vaughan Stream. It is an easy walk and well worth the time to see the twenty-foot Vaughan Falls. Time and mileage for this side trip have been budgeted into the hike.

From Vaughan Falls, return on the Appalachian Trail the way you came, half a mile back to the road. Turn right on the road, and walk .5 mile back to your car at Vaughan Stream.

Barren Mountain from Borestone summit

Chairback and Columbus Mountains

Total distance: 9.4 miles
Hiking time: 5 hours
Vertical rise: 2,100 feet
Maps: USGS 15' Sebec Lake; MATC 3 (1988)

Chairback and Columbus mountains stand five and six miles respectively south of Gulf Hagas on the Appalachian Trail (AT). They can be climbed from the same starting point as Gulf Hagas gorge, on the St. Regis Paper Company gravel road 7 miles west of Katahdin Iron Works. This hike makes a good companion hike to Gulf Hagas if you are camping in the area for a couple of days (Hike 26). Chairback and Columbus are in the Appalachian Trail's Hundred Mile Wilderness, which extends north from Monson to Abol Bridge at the southern boundary of Baxter State Park.

To get to the trailhead, travel ME 11 to a point 4 miles north of Brownville Junction. The sign "Katahdin Iron Works" indicates the 6.5-mile-long gravel road west to the remains of the iron works. This spot is a Maine State Historical Memorial with history and diagrams of the iron industry detailed on display boards. Although the area is now mostly uninhabited woodlands, in 1843 the settlement of Katahdin Iron Works was a thriving village with several hundred people, a hotel, and later a railroad. Iron ore was mined from Ore Mountain, a ridge 1.5 miles west, and carried by rail to the iron works for the roasting separation process. Several brick beehive charcoal ovens, of which one remains, prepared the charcoal used in the massive blast furnace, which still stands.

Next to the historical memorial stands

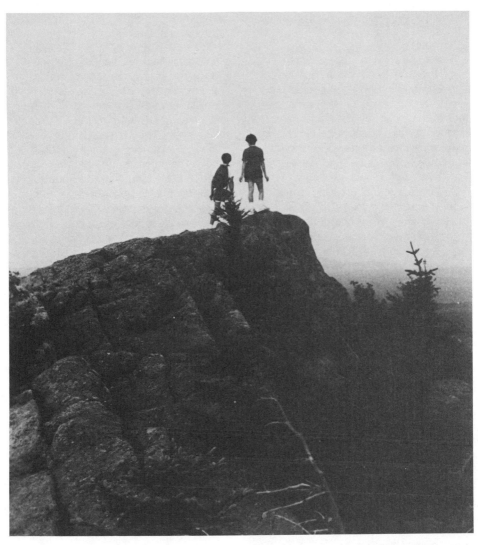

Hikers reach the summit of Chairback Mountain

the gatehouse at the entrance to the lands of Diamond International Company and St. Regis Paper Company. Here you need to register, pay a day-use or camping fee, ask for a Diamond Company map, and be admitted through the gate and across the bridge over the West Branch of the Pleasant River. From the bridge, take the right fork, and staying on the widest road, drive 7 miles to where the Appalachian Trail (sign) crosses the road at the bridge over a brook. (At 3.4 miles, be sure to fork left and cross the West

Branch of the Pleasant River.) Park well off the road, which is used by large logging trucks.

The Appalachian Trail follows the gravel road marked "Chairback Mountain Camps" uphill (south) beside the brook for a few yards, then turns left (east) away from the road and rises through maple, beech, and birch, some mature and quite large. On the ground you'll see hobblebush, wild sarsaparilla, rosy twisted-stalk, and wild oats.

At .6 mile the trail crosses an old woods road and ascends more steeply, crossing a dry brook through sunny woods carpeted with spinulose wood fern, wood sorrel, Indian cucumber, violets, and starflower. At 1.5 miles, a side trail leads .2 mile downhill to the shore of East Chairback Pond. The lovely pond teems with fish and some of the deepest-voiced bullfrogs I've heard.

From here the trail begins its steady ascent of Chairback Mountain through dense woods alternating with open woods, sheep laurel, blueberries, and then open slate ledges to the 2,197-foot summit, which offers a beautiful 180-de-gree panorama to the north. From left to right you see Gulf Hagas Mountain, West Peak, Hay, White Cap (Hike 27), and Saddleback mountains. Below to the west is East Chairback Pond.

A few minutes' descent takes you into a col, where you scramble 150 feet up white-blazed boulders to the Chairback Gap lean-to. The cozy setting in the col is only .5 mile from the summit of Columbus Mountain. Keep following white blazes beyond the lean-to through abundant clintonia lily and bunchberry to a ledge near the summit. (The actual summit is interior to the ledge and off the trail.) Another .2 mile through thick sheep laurel takes you to an overlook west to Long Pond. The overlook is marked with a large cairn.

From here you retrace the AT to your car. If you feel like swimming, stop halfway back to Katahdin Iron Works where the gravel road crosses the bridge over the West Branch of the Pleasant River. Swimming is particularly good here in the moderate current of a shallow bend in the river. Much of the river bed is sand, affording a nice beach.

Gulf Hagas

Total distance: 10 miles
Hiking time: 7 hours
Vertical rise: 600 feet
Maps: USGS 15' Sebec Lake; MATC 3 (1988); Diamond
  Company Map

Gulf Hagas, known as Maine's miniature Grand Canyon, is hidden in the Hundred Mile Wilderness of the Appalachian Trail, which extends from Monson to Abol Bridge. This scenic gorge is 7 miles west of historic Katahdin Iron Works, which is several miles northwest of Brownville and Brownville Junction. The West Branch of the Pleasant River has carved a slate canyon of sheer narrow walls up to 400 feet high, with numerous waterfalls and curious rock formations. The stream drops 500 feet through the 2.5-mile-long canyon, tumbling and frothing most of the way.

The Old Pleasant River Road, used in lumber operations a century ago, offers access to the Gulf from the east. The lands surrounding the Gulf are held by the St. Regis Paper Company and Diamond International Corporation. In 1968 Gulf Hagas was declared a Registered Natural Landmark in order to preserve its natural beauty. Chairback and Columbus mountains (Hike 25) and Gulf Hagas together make a fine two days of hiking in the same area. Although this hike is continually following water, there is no spring on this trail. You should begin with a full canteen.

To get to the trailhead, travel ME 11, 4 miles north from Brownville Junction, turn loft (west) at the Katahdin Iron Works sign, and drive 6.5 miles down a gravel road to the Iron works, which is a State Historical Memorial. (See Hike 25 for a description of Katahdin Iron Works.) After you register with the caretaker and pay a day-use or camping fee, you are provided with a Diamond Company map and admitted through the gate and across the bridge over the West Branch of the Pleasant River. (The USGS map is of limited usefulness here.) Beyond the bridge, take the right fork (stay on the widest road), bear left at the fork in 3.4 miles, and recross the West Branch of the Pleasant River. At 7 miles, the Appalachian Trail (AT) crosses this road at a bridge over a brook. Park well off the road, which is used by large logging trucks.

Follow the white blazes downhill to the right and north. (Directly opposite, the AT going south leads to Chairback and Columbus mountains, Hike 25.) You parallel the brook through a generally young beech and maple forest. At .7 mile ford the West Branch of the Pleasant River. Use caution on the slippery rocks. A stick will help you balance. In winter there is no problem on the frozen river; in early spring the water is likely to be too high to cross. As in all stream crossings, your backpack should be unbelted for quick removal in case you fall. Across the river, you begin walking through the Hermitage, a famous grove of beautiful white king pine, some 130 feet tall, now preserved by The Nature Conservancy of Maine. At 1 mile, you encounter the Old Pleasant River Road. Turn left (west) where a sign points to Screw Auger Falls. Shortly, you leave the Hermitage in mixed woods, mostly beech and maple. A variety of wildflowers dots the ground, such as clintonia lily, Canada mayflower, bunchberry, painted trillium, purple wakerobin, and wild sarsaparilla.

At 1.1 miles, in a clearing, the blueblazed 5.2-mile circuit trail to Gulf Hagas takes off straight ahead (north) while the white-blazed AT corners to the right (east) toward White Cap and Gulf Hagas mountains. Cross Gulf Hagas Brook on the blue-blazed trail to a boulder on

which a 1968 bronze plaque names Gulf Hagas a Registered Natural Landmark. From the boulder, a side trail leads .2 mile left to Screw Auger Falls, twenty-six feet high by four feet wide. The falls have worn and polished the rock into the shape of an S. This side trail should not be missed. Backtrack to the blue-blazed Gulf Hagas circuit trail, which continues north on the Old Pleasant River Road for .5 mile to an intersection marked by a painted rock, where you turn left downhill. (The circuit trail takes you back to this point, from which you return to your car the way you came.)

The trail drops south toward the West Branch of the Pleasant, with a side spur .2 mile south to Hammond Street Pitch. Peering down from this ninety-foot cliff of slate and sheep laurel, you will find it difficult in summer to see through the trees to the bottom of the gorge. Retrace the side spur back to the circuit trail and pull uphill past a couple of open view-points to Indian Head, the craggy profile of an Indian jutting out of

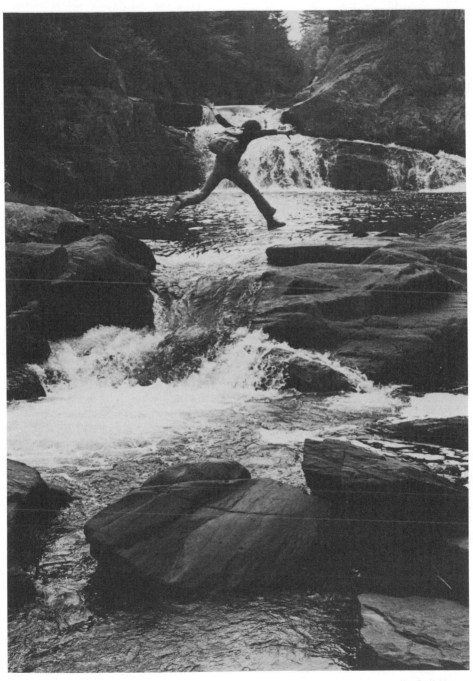

At Gulf Hagas

the canyon wall. This rock is on one side of the Lower Jaws, so named because an Indian log driver was killed there in a log jam in May 1882. Above at the Main Jaws, the channel was only some 7½ feet wide until a blast widened it to 26 feet. On the opposite south canyon wall, you can see white flowers of Labrador tea blooming in June and mountain ash's white flowers in June and its red berries in July and August. Beyond, four short spur trails provide downstream views of Lower and Main Jaws and upstream views of Upper Jaws.

Further, .3 mile above the Jaws, a side spur leads to a pool at the base of Buttermilk Falls, an appropriate name for the frothy, foaming water. The trail stays near the northern edge of the canyon for the next .5 mile, taking you past Stair Falls and Billings Falls, whose three bridal veils fall into a semicircular pool.

Gulf Hagas was carved by the West Branch of the Pleasant River, aided by river drivers' dynamite, out of rock known as the Carrabassett Formation. This rock type consists of shales, slates, and schists of the Devonian period, about 350 million years ago. The various falls occur where the river could not erode the rock away; thus, they stand as stumbling blocks impeding the river's course. It's a shame we can't see

such extraordinary beauty in all of life's stumbling blocks!

Shortly you reach the Head of the Gulf, where the river divides around an island and cascades toward you in step falls on both sides. This is the last overlook before the trail leaves the river and circles clockwise away from the Gulf and back to Old Pleasant River Road. You will pass on your left a road up the West Branch of the Pleasant to Lloyd Pond (where it crosses a main road should you wish to spot a car there) and on to Little Lyford Ponds. The trail takes you through dense spruce, marsh fern, jewelweed, hobblebush, and some large old maples, beech, and birch. The return trail is much faster, taking you past the painted rock, back to the side trail to Screw Auger Falls, and onto the white-blazed Appalachian Trail again, which you retrace to your car.

An important factor affecting the walking time of this hike is the ruggedness of the trail. Although there is not much measurable vertical rise during the 2.5 miles that the trail runs along the Gulf, every step you take is either up or down. There is no easy stride. The numerous spur trails to observation points add uncounted mileage to the hike. And you will want to stop, perhaps photograph, most definitely admire, the wonders of Gulf Hagas. Be sure you allow yourself ample time.

27

White Cap Mountain

Total distance: 5.2 miles / 8 miles
Hiking time: 4½ hours / 6 hours
Vertical rise: 2,200 feet
Maps: USGS 15' First Roach Pond, Jo-Mary Mountain; MATC
2 (1988)

White Cap, at 3,644 feet, is in the Hundred Mile Wilderness of the Appalachian Trail, is the trail's highest point between Katahdin and Bigelow, and is the highest peak in the Moosehead Lake region. On the open summit stands an abandoned Maine Forest Service firetower.

This is the only hike in the book that describes two trails to the summit. The White Brook Trail (5.2 miles, 4½ hours) is approached from Brownville Junction in central Maine. The West Branch Pond Trail (8 miles, 6 hours) begins closer to Greenville in western Maine. Although both trails meet on top of White Cap, their trailheads are half a day's drive apart. Not only can White Cap be climbed on a trip with Hikes 25 and 26, but it can also be climbed in a unit with Hikes 28–31 if you are spending time in the Moosehead Lake area.

I. White Brook Trail

The White Brook Trail is reached by driving ME 11 to a point 4 miles north of Brownville Junction. The sign "Katahdin Iron Works" indicates the 6.5-mile gravel road to the remains of the iron works. (For a description of the iron

works, see Hike 25, Chairback and Columbus.)

After you register with the caretaker and pay a day-use fee, you are provided with a Diamond Company map and admitted through the gate and across the bridge over the West Branch of the Pleasant River. Beyond the bridge, take the right fork, cross a smaller bridge, and pass Silver Lake on your right. Pass a right turn 2.3 miles from the gate at Katahdin Iron Works. At 3.5 miles, bear right at a fork, and at 5.9 miles, cross High Bridge over White Brook. At 6.1 miles pass a left turn to Gulf Hagas and the Hermitage, and at 7.3 miles take the left fork. The last leg is rough going, and you may need to park and walk if your car hasn't enough clearance. The road is firm on a gravel base, so there is no danger of becoming stuck; however, rocks or washouts may be a problem. At 9.6 miles the road crosses through a gravel pit, and at 9.9 miles a series of gullies will put a stop to your progress.

Park off the road and begin walking, following blue blazes. In about .5 mile, the gravel road ends, and the White Brook Trail continues to the left between two cairns at a trail sign. From here it is 2 miles to the summit of White Cap. You hike through a cutover area giving good open views. The young second growth offers prime moose habitat, verified by copious moose sign. Remnants of telephone wire along the trail show the former use of White Cap as a firetower peak. The trail soon leaves the cutover area and rises more steeply through spruce and fir. Half a mile from where you left the gravel road, the trail crosses the headwaters of White Brook in a beautiful glen where cascades keep the rocks wet, so be careful when crossing. Uphill from the brook, you reach a trail junction and the ruins of the former fire-warden's cabin. Take the trail which goes straight ahead. You are climbing through spruce and fir about fifty years old, but notice the size of some of the stumps of trees that were logged. Some stumps are ten times the size of the present growth!

Half a mile up from the cabin ruins, you crest the ridge between White Cap and Hay mountains at a junction with the Appalachian Trail (AT). To the left is Hay Mountain with Gulf Hagas beyond. Turn right, following the white-blazed AT for 1.1 mile to White Cap's summit. (Refer to the second hike description of White Cap for a summary of views from the summit.) To return to your car, hike the same trail in reverse.

II. West Branch Pond Trail

The western route to White Cap is approached from Greenville, on ME 15 at the southern tip of Moosehead Lake. From the blinking light in town, drive 17.8 miles north on the Ripogenus Road to a dirt road 1 mile south of Kokadjo. (You will pass Lily Bay State Park.) The dirt road is the Frenchtown or First

Roach Pond Road and is marked with a sign to West Branch Pond Camps. Turn right and drive carefully (the road is gravel and in bad condition) 10 miles to West Branch Pond Camps, passing many campsites along the shore of first Roach Pond. The Sterlings, who own and run the camps, offer parking space to hikers. Looking southeast over First West Branch Pond, you can see your destination: White Cap is the highest peak. To its right are Hay Mountain, West Peak, and Gulf Hagas Mountain, none of which are on this trail to White Cap. Parallel marks evident on the mountainsides are burns and skid roads, the results of logging operations. Active logging operations keep this trail in a state of change. Soon you may be able to drive much farther on the road before hiking, so it is a good idea to check at the camps before proceeding.

The trail leaves the northwest corner of the clearing where the camps are situated. With the pond on your left, walk between the cabins to the right rear corner of the clearing, in July, through meadow flowers: forget-me-nots, buttercups, and Queen Anne's lace. The path gets muddy as it enters a cedar and alder bog, where you begin to notice blue blazes on trees. At .2 mile, turn left at a fork onto a drier path through moosewood, hobblebush, wild sarsaparilla, and wood sorrel. Several yards later, you come out on the Mountain Road, which you walk to the left for .5 mile until it ends at the outlet where First West Branch Pond flows into the West Branch of the Plesant River. Here, a post is the only sign of a former bridge.

Cross the outlet by the post, stepping on stones to the opposite shore, cross a small flowage, and scramble up onto an old tote road. Turn left and follow the tote road through a corridor of alders, meadow rue, and meadowsweet. As the

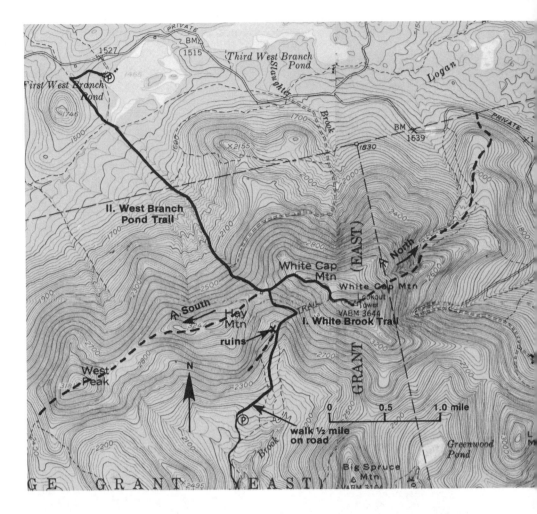

trail gains slight elevation, the growth changes to balsam fir, maple, and beech, under which grow thick raspberries, wild strawberries, buttercups, hawkweed, and yarrow. Follow blue blazes left onto another grass-grown road, moving south across a tributary to the West Branch of the Pleasant. Ascend through mixed hardwoods, paralleling the stream to the left. In spring, many ladyslippers bloom on this section of the trail, as well as clintonia lily, painted trillium, and starflower. Cross the stream,

and ascend more steeply southeast through more open woods abundant in hobblebush. Cross a dry stream bed and rise through dense young birch growth, across an old logging road. From here the ascent is very steep, through bunchberry and scrubby balsam fir.

The trail levels out at the crest of the ridge, joining the AT. To the right, the AT runs west toward Hay Mountain. Straight ahead, the White Brook Trail heads down the other side of the ridge.

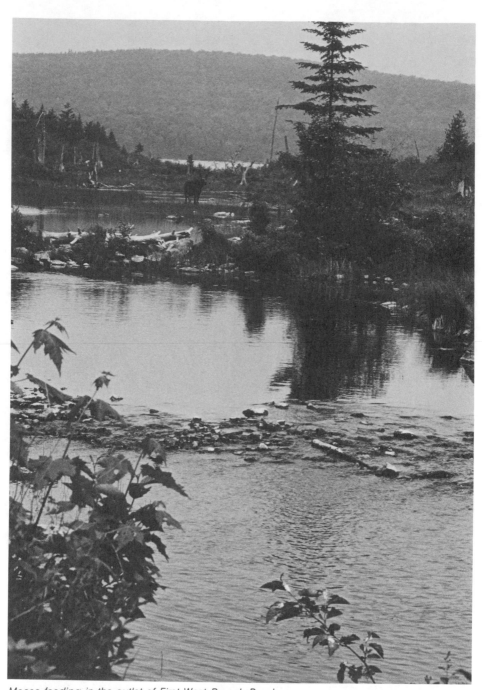

Moose feeding in the outlet of First West Branch Pond

Follow the AT to the left (northeast), 1.1 mile to the summit. You pass a spring and walk past clintonia lily, bunchberry, spinulose wood fern, wood sorrel, and an unusual clump of starflower. Most starflower grows one flower per stem. It is not unusual to see an occasional plant with two blooms twinned on one stem. However, in this clump almost all the flowers were twinned, and a few had three stars to a stem.

The trail runs along White Cap's ridge, dipping into a sag and back uphill through blueberries, bunchberry, Labrador tea, pale sheep laurel, and low scrub spruce. Mountain cranberry creeps over the summit rocks.

The abandoned tower is in poor condition but still standing on the slate and schist summit. Views from the summit are thrilling. To the north lie First, Second, and Third West Branch ponds with Second and Third Roach ponds behind. To the northeast, look over Big and Little Boardman mountains to Katahdin. The east is mountainous; highest is Jo-Mary Mountain. Southeast lies large, long Saddleback Mountain. Look south over Big Spruce Mountain to Chairback

and Columbus mountains (Hike 25), eastern peaks of the Barren-Chairback Range. From Chairback to the right are Columbus, Third, Fourth, and Barren (Hike 24) mountains. To the west is Hay Mountain with Baker Mountain behind. Northwest are Number Four Mountain and First Roach Pond, beyond which are Little Spencer Mountain, shaped like a whale, and Big Spencer Mountain (Hike 30), shaped like a box.

Return by the same trails to West Branch Pond Camps. If you have made a supper reservation, a pleasant evening awaits you in the dining cabin. I once spent a lovely summer evening at supper here. A storm gathered, darkening the sky and shrouding mist over White Cap and its identical but smaller unnamed companion pinnacle. Fish were rising to flies on First West Branch Pond, surrounded by blue flag iris in luxuriant bloom around the shore. A few raindrops began to fall, gathering to a brief but thorough summer shower and then tapering to clearing before the meal was over. The evening air was sweet and fresh after the rain.

Big Squaw

Total distance: 7 miles
Hiking time: 4 hours
Vertical rise: 2,000 feet
Map: USGS 15' Greenville

Big Squaw rises majestically over Moosehead Lake northwest of Greenville. It offers an aerial view of the lake from its summit, where the abandoned firetower stands on the site of the first fire lookout in the nation, established in 1905. The mountain was named for Maquaso, wife of the legendary Chief Kineo, who left him because of his wickedness and died on the mountain. Squaw Mountain Ski Area, now owned by the state of Maine, is on the east side of the mountain, but none of it can be seen from the summit or the hiking trail.

To reach the trailhead, drive 5.2 miles northwest from Greenville on ME 6-ME 15. Just before the road crosses Squaw Brook, a sign on the right marks the Maine Forest Service Squaw Brook Campsite, which is open to the public. Immediately after the highway crosses the brook, turn left at a sign onto a Scott Paper Company gravel road. One mile down this road is a turn around space on the left for parking. Across from the parking space, the trail (an old woods road) enters the woods to the southwest.

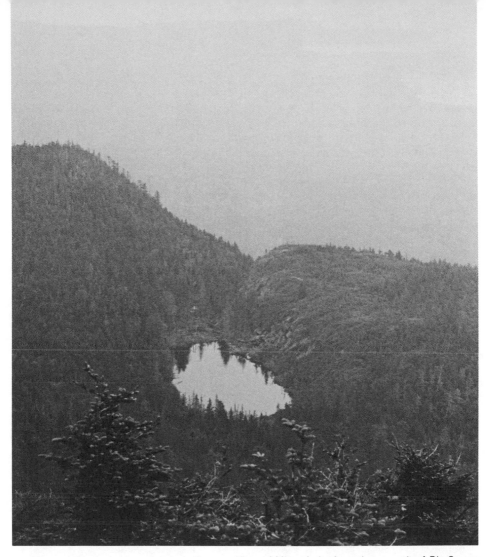

View of Mirror Lake from the summit of Big Squaw

There are no blazes, but the trail is worn and wide, rising only gradually. In July, near the beginning where the trail may be wet, blue flag iris grow among grasses in the center of the trail. Other summer flora are buttercup, cinquefoil, hawkweed, meadow rue, self-heal, wood sorrel, marsh fern, spinulose wood fern, and sensitive fern. Fauna on this trail are also abundant: families of partridge, red squirrels, song birds, and tracks of moose. The first half of the trail runs through mixed hardwoods, mostly beech and maple. When the trees become taller and the woods more open, you will see a stream on your left. The woods road ends as the trail angles left (west), crosses the stream, and heads uphill. As you rise higher, more birch and spruce appear among the maples, until soon the predominant growth is spruce, birch, and balsam fir.

At 2.5 miles you reach the empty warden's cabin, its dooryard filled with New

York fern and long beech fern. One hundred yards farther, you cross Squaw Brook and climb steep set-in stone steps, following the brook a short distance. The trail soon leaves the brook, swings north and then northeast, ascending more gently the last .5 mile to the summit through mature spruce and a forest floor of wildflowers. Note that the vegetation on top of the mountain, which has a shorter growing season, can be very different in timing from vegetation at the lower reaches. While summer flowers are in full bloom below, spring flowers such as Canada mayflower, trillium, and clintonia lily may still bloom at higher elevations. Later, fall flowers such as asters will bloom earlier above, while summer flowers are completing their longer cycle below.

The trail follows the exposed spine of the ridge the last few yards to the 3,196-foot summit. If you explore the summit, you might find garnets or black tourmalines. The west side of Big Squaw has large sheet deposits of mica.

The views from Big Squaw are famous for their variety. Spreading north and east are the hundreds of bays of Moosehead Lake, the largest lake east of the Mississippi within the boundary of one state. In Moosehead to the north, Mount Kineo (Hike 29) rises on a peninsula, and to the northeast you can see Big Spencer (Hike 31) and Katahdin (Hikes 33 and 34). To the east White Cap (Hike 27) and the Gulf Hagas Mountains form a citadel. Little Squaw Mountain stands close to the south. Southwest rise the horned peaks of Bigelow (Hike 13), and west is Coburn's gumdrop shape (Hike 20). Northwest beyond Squaw's ridge lies Brassua Lake and, behind it, Boundary Bald.

From the tower a short trail leads north, past a large clump of Labrador tea on your right, to a ledge with a view over Mirror Pond, a tarn high on the northeast spur of the mountain. Near the ledge you'll see more Labrador tea, whose clustered white flowers bloom in June and early July. The small dark green oval leaves with brown fuzz underneath can be picked, dried, and used for tea. In large enough quantities the tea is a laxative.

Return to the firetower, where you retrace the trail past the warden's camp and down to your car.

At the time of this writing, new trails were being developed on and around Little Squaw Mountain, just south of Big Squaw. Little Squaw is now a state recreation area owned by the Bureau of Public Lands. You might want to investigate these new hikes.

Mount Kineo

Total distance: 4 miles
Hiking time: 2½ hours
Vertical rise: 800 feet
Map: USGS 7.5' Brassua Lake East; USGS 15' Moosehead
  Lake, Brassua Lake

Mount Kineo is a cliff-hanger of a hike up a mountain in the middle of Moosehead Lake. It stands on a peninsula that is almost an island, projecting from Moosehead's eastern shore across North Bay to within 1 mile of the western shore at Rockwood. Views from the abandoned Maine Forest Service tower on the summit sweep all of Moosehead Lake, the largest lake within the boundary of a single state east of the Mississippi. There are no public roads to Mount Kineo; the only approach is from the water. If you do not have your own canoe, you can rent one from any of several places in Rockwood.

Rockwood is 30 miles east of Jackman and 20 miles northwest of Greenville on ME 6-ME 15. In Rockwood, turn north off ME 6-ME 15 on the only road that turns north down to the lakeshore and Rockwood Village. This road passes Whitten's Store, where you can rent a canoe, and the post office. From the post office, turn onto a dirt road and drive a few yards to the public boat launch on the lake. A parking fee is charged.

The canoe trip should be made only in good weather; a gale on a lake as

large as Moosehead could resemble a storm at sea. Paddle northeast toward Mount Kineo. You can beach and leave your craft anywhere along Kineo's south shore and intersect the shore path as it skirts Kineo. However, the hiking mileage will start at the dock at Kineo Cove, which you reach by skirting the shore around to the right and entering the cove by the Mount Kineo Hotel. From the cove you can see the sheer east face, below which is the deepest place in all of Moosehead Lake, the 250-foot Kineo Deep Hole.

From the Kineo Cove dock, walk the dirt road past the eastern edge of the golf course, staying left at any forks and passing open fields that used to be sheep pastures, until you reach the path at the water's edge on the south shore. Walk the shore path westward through alders and birches, under towering cliffs of Kineo flint and past the remains of an avalanche, to the southwest point of land, .6 mile from the dock. Here you leave the lake. There is no water on the mountain, except an intermittent spring near the top.

The Indian Trail leaves to the right, straight uphill northeast into a grove of red pines. There is no sign, but the trail is worn, and there are occasional blue blazes. Ascend stratified layers of sandstone, shale, and quartzite almost like steps. When you reach the top of the first cliff, you pass a side trail that leads back toward the hotel. In spite of all the cliff-climbing, no handholds are necessary on this hike. You walk above the avalanche remains that you saw from below, along bearberry-covered cliffs, and then ascend into woods of red oak and maple.

When you come back out onto ledges again, views are southeast to the hotel, golf course, and fields where sheep once grazed. This southeast end of Kineo is volcanic Kineo rhyolite. The mountain was formed from a contact of volcanic rhyolite and sandstone, shale,

and quartzite. The trail alternates between sheer cliffs and woods. The last time you leave the open cliffs, at .9 mile, notice a trail that drops into the woods on your left as you enter the woods. There is no sign. This will be your return circuit; it is the Bridle Trial.

After passing the Bridle Trail on your left, you ascend to the top of a rise and down into a small valley of spinulose wood fern, bracken fern, Canada mayflower, bunchberry, and wood sorrel. The change from cliffs to woods is extreme. Suddenly you could be in the middle of the Maine woods instead of in the middle of a lake.

Ascend gradually northeast to a fork in the trail. (To the right the trail runs a few yards to the former fire warden's tiny decrepit emergency shelter.) Bear left and walk a few yards to the tower on the wooded 1,789-foot summit. The tower offers spectacular views in all directions.

Look south over Moosehead Lake to Big Squaw (Hike 31), named after the wife of legendary Chief Kineo, southwest to Long Pond, closer southwest over the shoulder of Kineo to Blue Ridge, the only sharp hill across the lake in Rockwood, and beyond to the right to Coburn Mountain (Hike 20). To the west, the Moose River flows east out of Brassua Lake, past Rockwood, and into Moosehead Lake. To the northwest, Boundary Bald Mountain rises above Jackman eight miles from the Quebec border. To the north, Moosehead ends in Seboomook Cove and northeast at Northeast Carry. Look east-northeast over Little Kineo Mountain to Lobster Mountain, and east over Little Spencer, shaped like an inverted kettle, to Big Spencer Mountain (Hike 31). Southeast beyond Cowan Cove is Spencer Bay, backed by Number Four Mountain and the Lily Bay Mountains.

View of Mount Kineo from Rockwood

From the tower you can trace the entire Moosehead Lake traverse made by Henry David Thoreau on July 25, 1857, detailed in *The Maine Woods*. Starting in Greenville near Big Squaw Mountain, Thoreau and his Indian guide paddled forty miles across the lake in a sixteen-foot birchbark canoe with about one foot of freeboard (clearance above water). It took them eight hours to paddle the twenty miles to Kineo, a trip that takes most people two days. They stopped overnight, climbed Mount Kineo, and continued from there twenty more miles to Northeast Carry.

You are also looking at most of the watershed of the upper Kennebec River. Another interesting feature is the route taken by the quaternary (the most recent) glacier through this area. Blue Ridge to the southwest and Little Kineo Mountain to the northeast are in perfect alignment, with Kineo at the center. These three mountains form one straight ridge. All are smooth-sloped on their northwest faces, the side from which the glacier approached and pushed against the long ridge. Correspondingly, all three have a sheer vertical southeast face that resulted from the back-eddying (known as plucking or quarrying) of the glacier as it tumbled over the peak. Thoreau described the east face of Kineo on an earlier trip in 1853: "The celebrated precipice is so high and perpendicular that you can jump from the top, many hundred feet, into the water. . . . Probably it will be discovered that some Indian maiden jumped off it for love once, for true love never could have found a path more to its mind."

Indian lore is rich with legends concerning Mount Kineo. The mountain was named for Chief Kineo, a wicked Indian leader who was exiled by his tribe and lived on the mountain. One legend claims that the mountain is the petrified body of a moose killed by Glooskap, from Indian mythology. The word in Abnaki means "sharp peak."

Leave the tower and retrace .3 mile of the trail. Just before the trail emerges onto the first open ledges, the Bridle Trail (no sign) drops into the woods away from the cliffs, first through spruce and fir, and then through maple, white and yellow birch, Canada mayflower, clintonia lily, rosy twisted-stalk, club moss, purple wake-robin, wild sarsaparilla, and white aster. The trail descends to the former fire warden's cabin on the lakeshore, turns left behind the cabin, and runs out onto the shore path. From here, follow the shore path south back towards the hotel. In .3 mile you pass on your left the Indian Trail, which you climbed up the mountain. From here it is .6 mile back to the hotel.

(The shore path extends north beyond the fire warden's cabin a little over 1 mile to Hardscrabble Point, where there is a state-authorized campsite.)

Kineo has long held two positions: summer tourist haven and overseer of logging operations. Kineo has stood watch over two centuries of logging and log driving. Logging hit its record high in the 1890s and ended with the Last Log Drive in the summer of 1976, when log driving by water was declared illegal.

As a tourist center, Kineo was visited in the nineteenth century by summer people who came with steamer trunks and horses to the two or three hotels and often stayed for two months. They arrived by the Somerset Railway from Bingham, or by buckboard, and finally by lake steamer. The *Katahdin* was the last of these steamers, later used by the Scott Paper Company to tow logs, and is now a museum in Greenville. The hotels often burned down and were rebuilt. From 1900 into the 1920s, Kineo was in its heyday of summer activity, complete with fishing guides, boating, golf, and elegant hotels. Recent years have seen changes. In the 1960s Kineo became a private club with forty-eight lots and owners. Before many of the plans to build had materialized, the 1973 energy crisis ended the endeavor to develop Kineo, and the future of the peninsula has been in limbo ever since.

Green Mountain

Total distance: 3 miles
Hiking time: 1½ hours
Verticle rise: 600 feet
Maps: USGS 15' Penobscot Lake; North Maine Woods Map

Green Mountain, northwest of Moose-head Lake and near the Canadian border, is appropriately named. It is forested with large old hardwoods, predominantly rock (sugar) maple. Except during the fall blaze of color, the trail is canopied with lovely green leaves of tall maples. This hike is especially beautiful in early spring, around Memorial Day, when the entire trail is carpeted with wildflowers. Mr. Ray Hearn, former fire warden, for many years kept the trail immaculately groomed. The hike is a walk through an enchanted forest, to a tower that affords exceptional views.

The mountain is far in the north woods of Somerset County on Great Northern Paper Company land northwest of Pittston Farm. Your car should be dependable with an odometer that works. Starting on ME 6-ME 15 at Rockwood (30 miles east of Jackman and 20 miles northwest of Greenville) cross the Moose River bridge and fork right onto the Great Northern dirt road that leads 20 miles north to Pittston Farm at the west end of Seboomook Lake. You must register at a gate shortly before arriving at Pittston Farm. Pass Pittston Farm and stop at the Maine Forest Service (MFS) ranger station just beyond it on the left.

Here you can obtain a *Sportsman's Map of the North Maine Woods* and confirm the directions to Green Mountain. Paper company roads are always changing—new roads are built, and old roads are discontinued—sometimes confusing travelers. (See Aroostook County Introduction, page 176, for more information on the North Maine Woods.) You should carry water on this hike.

From the MFS station, drive .2 mile and bear right at the fork. At 1.6 miles pass the MFS Lane Brook Campsite on the left, at 1.9 miles fork left, at 4.3 miles fork right, at 5.8 miles fork right, and at 6.4 miles fork left. At 8.7 miles, you will see a sign at the Green Mountain trailhead, which begins by the driveway to the ranger's cabin. Park off the road and walk to the cabin.

In the cabin dooryard and driveway in May you can see Dutchman's-breeches, a rare wildflower that blooms in abundance here. Around the cabin, yellow, blue, and white violets carpet the ground in June.

The trail turns left behind the cabin and heads generally north for 1.5 miles to the summit tower. Beginning in a boggy area, the trail takes you through violets, Canada mayflower, rosy twisted-stalk, clintonia lily, hobblebush, bunchberry, starflower, and trillium. The path is beautifully groomed and the sugar (rock) maples spread their canopy far above you, inspiring reverence. The trail ascends at an easy grade through wood sorrel and Indian cucumber, rosy twisted-stalk, patchwork mosses, and bracken fern. Rosy twisted-stalk is a charming member of the lily family. Its zigzag stem supports alternate pointed leaves, each with a tiny pink bell-shaped flower hanging under it. Now and then on the trail, outcroppings of pure white milky quartz are visible, and occasionally you can see a clump of Indian pipe. The last .5 mile is steeper as you mount the wooded summit to the sixty-foot steel tower. You will retrace this trail to return to your car.

The summit tower offers views of the northwestern Maine wilderness to Mount Katahdin fifty-eight miles east, and over pastoral Quebec with its farms and villages. Far to the north-northeast looms the conical peak of Allagash Mountain on Allagash Lake. Northeast beyond the North Branch of the Penobscot lie the five St. John ponds. Look east over Lane Pond to Foley Pond and Mount Katahdin on the horizon, and southeast to Seboomook Lake and beyond to Big Spencer Mountain on the left (Hike 31) and Big Squaw on the right (Hike 28). To the south-southeast, Ironbound Mountain rises behind Canada Falls Lake and in front of Brassua Lake. Look south over the South Branch of the Penobscot to Long Pond and south-southwest to Boundary Bald Mountain,

Ranger Ray Hearn sharpens a scythe to groom the Green Mountain trail

beyond which Sugarloaf (Hike 48) and Bigelow (Hike 13) can be seen seventy miles away. South is Coburn Mountain (Hike 20). Look west over Long Pond and Penobscot Lake into Canada. To the northwest, it is twenty-six miles to Canada, where clear-cutting on the Canadian side defines quite visibly the international border. You can see thirty miles to the farmland, villages, and Catholic church spires of Quebec.

While you are in the area, there are some interesting side trips you may want to take. The ranger at the MFS station on the access road can direct you to Little Russell Mountain, a tedious but beautiful drive north up the Caucomgomac Road, for a 3-mile hike to and from an old fire tower. This trail is just over 1.2 miles beyond Lost Pond Campsite, a beautiful place to camp by a fly-fishing-only pond. The walk-in campsite is .2 mile off the road.

Directly south of Little Russell Mountain is the town of Seboomook, located between the east end of Seboomook Lake and the Northwest Carry of Moosehead Lake. Today Seboomook amounts to some private camps, a campground, and a store, but at one time it had a large tourist hotel, the Seboomook House. During World War II, from 1944 to 1946, Seboomook also was the site of a prisoner-of-war camp for 250 German soldiers captured in Africa. At the store you can see photographs of the camp, its three sentry towers, barracks, mess hall, cell block, infirmary, ice house, ration building, staff house, PX, and recreation building. Now only the foundations and the chimney of the mess hall remain. Using horses, the prisoners cut and drove softwood into Seboomook Lake, through the dam, into the West Branch of the Penobscot, past Lobster Lake, and into Chesuncook Lake. They worked hard, were paid, and were treated well. After they were returned to Germany, some of them came back to work for Great Northern, and today many still return with their families to camp at Seboomook.

Pittston Farm, directly on your way back to Rockwood from Green Mountain, is also worth a stop. It is located at the head of Seboomook Lake (west end), where the North and South Forks come together to form the West Branch of the Penobscot River. Its history begins with the clearing of roads through the wilderness in the 1830s for the passage of troops to the Canadian border. Here the "Old Canada Tote Road" crossed the South Branch of the Penobscot at the site of Pittston Farm, but it was never used for military purposes. In the 1850s woodsmen and river drivers used a log cabin built here by a

man named Knight. In 1900 more land was cleared, and five or six more log buildings were built. In 1906 Great Northern bought this area, known as Pittston Township, from the owners, the Holyoke family of Brewer, Maine, and the 100-acre farm became headquarters for cutting operations on the North and South Branches of the Penobscot.

From 1908 to 1913 the farm took on its appearance today. Buildings were frame construction on concrete or masonry foundations and housed workers, executives, and guests of Great Northern. There were stables, a blacksmith shop, a wagon shed, a storehouse, a boarding house, an ice house, barns, water works, a potato house, an office, a hen house, a cannery, and a slaughter house. In 1913 the construction of Seboomook dam (rebuilt in the winter of 1926–1927) flooded the lower land, destroying the original log buildings. From 1914 to the late 1950s, Pittston Farm also served as the central telephone switchboard in the area, linking remote areas of Maine with the telephone and telegraph system of the rest of the country.

From the early twentieth century to the late 1930s, men stayed at the farm, going to and coming from woods operations and river drives. Enough produce was raised to supply all operations in the area. Pittston Farm was no longer an isolated frontier stopover for woodsmen as in the nineteenth century, but as comfortable as a resort. Running water, electricity, steam heat, telephones, daily mail service, white paint, bed sheets, and a lounge equipped with magazines and newspapers, playing cards, stationery, and a victrola were among its comforts. Woodsmen and laborers slept in the third-floor "ram's pastures" of the two lodges, while superintendents, paymasters, clerks, and visitors—tourists, hunters, and fishermen—occupied the second-story rooms.

Truck transportation and bulldozed roads brought about the decline of Pittston Farm's importance, and farming was discontinued. When river driving ended in 1971, Pittston Farm was shut down. Today some of the buildings are gone, but most remain, maintained by the Great Northern Paper Company and used occasionally for special purposes. All summer long, the farm bustles with Boy Scouts from all over the United States. Since 1973, it has been the Seboomook Base, center for the Maine National High Adventure Program, Boy Scouts of America. The old potato house now houses canoes and other equipment, gear and trail food, a trading post, and an exhibit of old tools. Staff and scouts live in tents in the fields and woods.

Although Pittston Farm no longer offers luxury accommodations, visitors are always welcome. A stop can give you an interesting perspective on history and geography in the area of Green Mountain.

31

Big Spencer

Total distance: 4 miles
Hiking time; 2 hours
Vertical rise: 2,000 feet
Map: USGS 7.5' Big Spencer Mountain; USGS 15' Ragged
  Lake

Big Spencer and its close neighbor Little Spencer rise high over wild lake country in western Piscataquis County. The tower offers the best views of Maine's big lakes west of Katahdin and south of the Allagash. You can see the whole

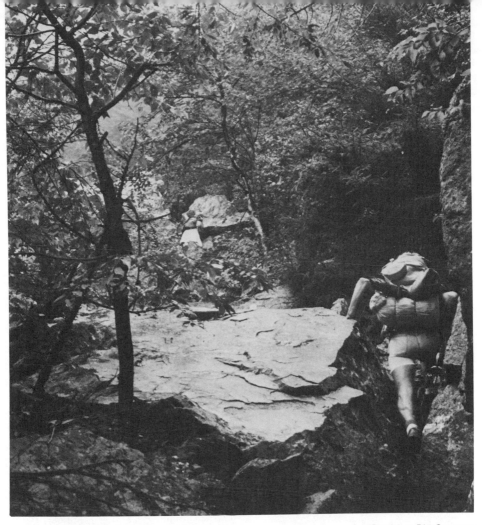

forty-mile length of Moosehead and the thirty-mile length of Chesuncook Lake. Many of Maine's highest mountains ring the horizon.

From the blinking light in downtown Greenville, at the southern tip of Moosehead, leave ME 6-ME 15 and drive north on the Ripogenus Road 19 miles to Kokadjo. Bear left at the fork .2 mile beyond Kokadjo, and 5 miles beyond Kokadjo check in at the Siras Gate of the Great Northern Company. In another 3.2 miles (2 miles southwest of Grant Farm) turn left (northwest) on a side road just after the Maine Forest Service (MFS) Bear Brook Campsite. Driving from Kokadjo, you can see the two-mile ridge of Big Spencer on your left, stretching northeast to southwest. After the turn at Bear Brook Campsite, drive 6 miles, forking right at 1.4 miles and left at 2.5 miles. At 6.1 miles, the trail (a woods road) takes off left (south). Park at the trailhead.

The first .5 mile rises gently through spruce, birch, beech, and maple. The unused road offers sign of moose and deer. (At .4 mile, a trail comes in from the left and joins the trail to Big Spencer.) Keep walking uphill, more steeply now, through trillium, rosy twisted-stalk, Canada mayflower, and wood sorrel. The trail abounds with Indian cucumber, a single-stemmed plant one- to three-feet tall with a small circlet of three to four leaves at the top and a larger rosette of six to ten pointed oval leaves midway down the stem. At the top, tiny greenish-yellow flowers dangle in spring, maturing to dark blue berries in fall when the upper leaves are tinged with red. The root of Indian cucumber is an edible tuber with a sweet, succulent, earthy taste resembling that of a cucumber. The root cannot be pulled up by the stem; it must be dug with fingers.

The trail rises through mixed hardwoods with many striped maples, passes the fire warden's cabin, levels out in open spruce-birch woods, and crosses a brook into the forest ranger's cabin site at 1.3 miles. From the cabin, views north and east are splendid. Look north over Blood Pond to Blackcap Mountain, east to Ragged Lake, and beyond to Caribou Lake, which opens into Chesuncook Lake. East behind the lakes stands Katahdin, showing you its Hunt Spur where the Appalachian Trail ascends to the Tableland and Baxter Peak. You can also see the many slides on Mount O-J-I (Hike 38) left of Katahdin with the cap of Mount Coe behind it. The tallest mountain behind O-J-I is the North Brother (Hike 39), and the low mountain in the midground is Sentinel (Hike 37). The leftmost of the big Baxter Park mountains are Doubletop (Hike 40) in front and The Traveler behind (Hike 44). To the northwest is Lobster Lake.

South behind the cabin, the summit looks like the volcano it was 400 million years ago, now eroded down to the mere roots of its former hulk. The trail is unblazed but easy to follow. Leave from behind the cabin, crossing an icy spring-fed brook, and begin the steep and rocky .7-mile ascent. The trail curves southwest and south, rising through some large red spruce, balsam fir, mountain ash, blueberries, mountain cranberries, and lots of large boulders. Ladders are placed at various spots to be helpful. Near the top, you ascend several ladders through dwarfed red spruce, Labrador tea, and sheep laurel to the rocky open northeast summit, 3,230 feet in elevation, and composed of volcanic rhyolite. (From cabin to tower you gain 1,000 vertical feet in .7 mile.)

The tower, erected in 1917, is operated by MFS watchman John Boydston, as of this writing. Views sweep over vast lake country, north-east over Ragged Lake, past Sentinel Mountain to Katahdin, and east-southeast over Farrar Mountain to Jo-Mary Mountain. Southeast behind Shaw Mountain is White Cap (Hike 27) and to its right are Hay, West Peak, and Gulf Hagas mountains. South beyond First Roach Pond is Number Four Mountain, and beyond, Lily Bay Mountain and Baker Mountain. To the south is Greenville on Moosehead Lake, where you can see ski slopes on Big Squaw (Hike 28). Southwest rises Little Spencer Mountain close by, and Mount Kineo (Hike 29) beyond. Past Kineo you can see the thin line of Brassua Lake. West-southwest beyond Kidney Pond lies Moosehead Lake, and behind it rises Boundary Bald Mountain on the Canadian border. Northwest is Lobster Lake, and north are Blood Pond, Blackcap Mountain, and Ragged, Caribou, and Chesuncook lakes.

Take the same trail back to the cabin and trailhead. It is much easier going down!

Baxter State Park

INTRODUCTION

Officially established in 1933, Baxter State Park covers 314 square miles in north-central Maine. From 1930 to 1962, Percival Baxter, governor of Maine from 1920 to 1925, made gifts of land to the state with the stipulation that the area remain "forever wild." Mile-high Mount Katahdin, a granite monolith and Maine's highest mountain, rises in the southern half of the park, surrounded by the Cross Range and other peaks at the northern end of the 500-million-year-old Appalachian Mountain range. Numerous streams and ponds are scattered at its base. The northern half of Baxter Park features South Branch Pond and The Traveler, a large volcanic mountain with radiating arms like a starfish. Central in the park's interior are Russell Pond and Wassataquoik Lake. Numerous trails crisscross Katahdin, and several longer trails course through the entire park, disclosing many wonders: waterfalls, mountain peaks, trout ponds, wildflowers, and historical sites.

In this guide, Baxter State Park is the location for fourteen day hikes (Hikes 32–45), and two backpacking trips (Hike 49, Webster Lake Trail; and Hike 50, Russell Pond).

Campsites and lean-tos in Baxter Park are limited in number to control the number of people using the park at one time. Reservations should be made in writing and paid for in advance. It is risky to plan on arriving and finding a vacancy. Write and send fees to Reservation Clerk, Baxter State Park Office, 64 Balsam Drive, Millinocket, ME 04462. Familiarity with park regulations is very important. Among other rules, no pets are admitted, and there is a size limit on vehicles, because of narrow park roads. There is no need for a reservation if you enter the park for day-use only. From the Millinocket office you can also purchase an excellent guidebook and/or map of the entire park, Steven Clark's map and *Guide to Baxter State Park and Katahdin.* Smaller, less detailed maps issued at the park gates are adequate for trails, and USGS maps are especially good for identifications.

A less-used gate, West Gate, provides access to the park at Nesowadnehunk Lake. This gate is not useful for hikes in this book.

Most-often used is the southeastern Togue Pond Gate, the access for Hikes 32–40 and 50. The gate is approached from Millinocket, which is reached from the Medway exit of Interstate 95, about eighty miles north of Bangor. The Great Northern Paper Company has a large mill west of the town and another in East Millinocket. Daily tours of the mill are open to the public. Gasoline and groceries should be obtained in Millinocket.

From Millinocket, follow signs north 9 miles to Millinocket Lake, where you will find a small store with gas pump and telephone, a campground, float plane service, and a public beach on the lake. From Millinocket Lake it is 6.5 miles to an important fork. The gravel Baxter State Park Road forks right, while the tarred road to the left passes Abol Bridge over the West Branch of the Penobscot, goes to Ripogenus Dam, and reaches Greenville 58 miles from this point. Take the right fork and drive 1.5 miles to Togue Pond Campground and, just beyond it, the Togue Pond Gate into Baxter Park.

The Matagamon Gate is the northeast entrance of the park (access to Hikes 41–45 and 49), approached from the town of Patten. Drive Interstate 95 about 90 miles north of Bangor to the Sherman exit. Follow ME 159-ME 11 through Sherman to Patten, a farming community in the potato belt of northern Penobscot County. Gasoline and groceries should be obtained here, and, if time permits, a visit to the Lumberman's Museum north of town is exciting and educational. It has interesting displays of equipment, including an old Lombard Steam Tractor, models of old lumber camps showing how lumbermen and log drivers lived, and a complete sawmill.

From Patten, drive ME 159 northwest 10 miles to Shin Pond, where you will see a small store and float plane service. Beyond, follow the Grand Lake Road, named for Grand Lake Matagamon. You cross the Seboeis River 16 miles from Patten and the East Branch of the Penobscot in 26 miles, where you'll see a small store with gas pump and a campground. The Matagamon Gate to Baxter State Park is 1 mile farther.

Once in the park, you will follow the Baxter State Park Road (also called the Park Perimeter Road), which makes a three-quarter circle through the park. A section of the Baxter State Park Road still bears its original name, "Nesowadnehunk Tote Road." It is a narrow gravel woods road offering few views.

Baxter is open for general use from May 15 to October 15 each year, and from October 15 to December 1 and April 1 to May 15 for day-use only. Permits may be necessary to hike in Baxter at times other than during the main May to October season. Contact Baxter Park authorities *before* planning an off-season trip.

Winter use for cross-country skiing and backpacking is becoming increasingly popular. Maintaining close contact with authorities and following the stringent winter regulations are necessary to ensure a safe adventure. Budget plenty of time for planning, and be sure to include someone with winter camping experience on a trip of this nature.

32

South Turner Mountain

Total distance (round trip): 4 miles
Hiking time: 3½ hours
Vertical rise: 1,630 feet
Maps: USGS 7.5' Katahdin Lake; USGS 15' Katahdin; Baxter
Park Map

The writers of the *Guide to the Appalachian Trail in Maine* suggest that the panoramic view from the top of South Turner ranks second only to that of Katahdin, and we are hard put to argue with them. Turner is an unusual gem of a mountain, affording a nearly perfect vista of the eastern portion of Baxter State Park. South Turner will also treat you to splendid views to the South, Great, North, and Little North basins of Katahdin.

To make the ascent of South Turner, head west from Millinocket on the Millinocket-Greenville Road and enter the park via Togue Pond Gate. Just beyond the Togue Pond Gatehouse, turn right and follow a gravel road 7.3 miles north to Roaring Brook Campground. The South Turner trail begins at the camping area. You'll usually find plenty of room for overnighting here, but reservations are necessary, particularly at the height of the summer. (See Baxter State Park: Introduction.)

The trail heads due north from the parking lot at the ranger station and follows the Russell Pond Trail for a short distance. Cross Roaring Brook and continue straight ahead on the Sandy Stream Pond Trail when the Russell Pond Trail turns left. You walk on the level to the left of an outlet stream from Sandy Stream Pond, cross an outlet brook, and then begin to skirt the southeast shore of the pond at just over .3 mile. This is moose country, and sightings are frequent. You will be more likely to see one of the large creatures on your descent, around sundown.

At approximately .7 mile from the trailhead, you'll reach a junction where Sandy Stream Pond Trail curves to the left around the pond. Turn right here on South Turner Mountain Trail on a level stretch through a field of boulders and stands of mixed hardwoods. At slightly over a mile, the grade steepens as you continue generally northeastward. A short trail on the right to a brook is passed at just over 1.5 miles.

Not long after passing the brook side trail, you emerge from the scrub and get a taste of the fine views that prevail on the upper limits of the mountain. The going is over ledges on a ridge from here to the summit. Especially when visibility is poor, keep your eye open for blue blazes on the rock. The scramble up the ledges ends on the summit at 2 miles from Roaring Brook.

From South Turner's open, rocky apex you can look northeast over the high tableland that connects this elevation with North and East Turner mountains. Katahdin Lake stretches out to the southeast, while the Whidden Ponds are immediately below to the west. Fine views take in the Russell Pond area to the northwest. The full spectacular expanse of Katahdin is to the west, between Abol and Rum mountains in the south and Russell Mountain in the north. A copy of the 15′ USGS Katahdin quadrangle makes a good addition to your pack on this trip to help you identify the many peaks visible from South Turner.

South Turner Mountain was born as a part of Mount Katahdin 360 million years ago when a vast dome of molten magma intruded from underground, pushing up the land above it like a blister. As the melted rock cooled, crystals solidified, producing the Katahdin granite unit, a mixture of quartz, feldspar, and mica.

The granite exposed near South Turner's summit looks different from the rock on Mount Katahdin, even though they came from one mass. The individ-

Blooming Diapensia, *a tundra plant, in a crevice on South Turner Mountain*

ual mineral grains in the rock on South Turner are much smaller and more difficult to single out, giving the granite a sugary appearance. Mount Katahdin's granite, with its large, obvious mineral grains, probably cooled more slowly, at greater depths in the earth, whereas the finer-grained South Turner outcrops must have experienced more rapid cooling.

Since the creation of this huge mass of granite, erosion has carved it into the various granite mountains here today, such as Katahdin, Turner, Doubletop, O-J-I, and the Brothers. Mount Katahdin is perhaps only one-third the original height of this granite body.

The descent from the mountain retraces your route in, keeping left at the east end of Sandy Stream Pond. You may vary the return if you wish by turning right at Sandy Stream Pond and following the trail north and west to its junction with the Russell Pond Trail. Bear left on the Russell Pond Trail and head south to Roaring Brook. This variation is somewhat longer than heading back directly along the pond's southeast shore.

Katahdin: Pamola, The Knife Edge, Chimney, South, and Baxter Peaks

Total distance (round trip): 9.8 miles
Hiking time: 8 hours
Vertical rise: 3,700 feet
Maps: USGS 7.5' Mount Katahdin; USGS 15' Katahdin; Baxter
 Park Map; MATC 1 (1988)

The Helon Taylor Trail, named after
H.N. Taylor who was for many years
Baxter Park's superintendent, provides a
dramatic 3,400-foot ascent up Keep
Ridge to Pamola, the Knife Edge, and
the rest of Katahdin's highest peaks.
There are outstanding views along the
route's entire length, and the hiker has
opportunities to experience stretches of
mountain terrain (on the Knife Edge)
found nowhere else in the East. This
hike, as could be expected on an ascent of Maine's highest mountain, will
test your endurance a little. The trail demands steady work on the ascent and
will test your brakes on the way down.

Begin your climb at Roaring Brook
Campground, which is reached on a
gravel road about 8 miles north of the
Togue Pond Gatehouse. Because parking is limited, you should arrive before
8:00 A.M. during the peak summer and
fall season. When the parking lot is full,
the trail is closed to hiking. You can also
camp at Roaring Brook by reservation.
Hikers should register with the ranger at
Roaring Brook before starting out on the
trail and *again* on their return. This
hikers' log helps keep tabs on foot traffic

on the great expanse of Katahdin, in
case rescue is needed.

Keep Ridge and the peaks of Katahdin are exposed to high winds, so
carry extra clothing with you even if the
weather seems mild. Windshells,
sweaters, rainwear, a hat, and gloves
belong in your rucksack. You should
also take along ample food. Roaring
Brook is the only sure place to fill canteens for six hot strenuous miles of
climbing; so be sure to carry plenty of
water.

The Taylor Trail departs from the
Chimney Pond Trail .1 mile from Roaring Brook Campground, following Keep
Ridge, named for Reverend Marcus
Keep who first opened the trail on this
ridge in the 1840s. You hike to the west,
climbing rapidly to a bare spot (Ed's
Lookout) in .3 mile. The trail levels off
momentarily here, and there are good
views to the ridges higher up. Passing
through scrub growth and boulders, you
continue on nearly level ground to the
southwest and west.

One mile above Roaring Brook, you
begin to climb more steeply again, moving out of birch growth, and then de-

scend briefly to the bed of Bear Brook at 1.3 miles. After passing groves of spruce and balsam, you move more out into the open, climbing on a pronounced grade. Views of the mountains and ponds in the southeast corner of Baxter Park are frequent from this section of Keep Ridge.

Continuing upward, you hike through more boulders above the 2-mile point and along the bare ridge. The route levels off again for a moment 2.5 miles from the road by a large boulder, where excellent views of Pamola, Chimney Peak, and the Knife Edge are ahead to the west. The route ahead lies in the open but can be lost in cloud and wind; thus caution should be used if the weather turns inclement. The summit of Pamola is reached 3.2 miles from your starting point.

Pamola looks down on deep, rocky South Basin and tiny Chimney Pond. It also provides an excellent lookout over the north ridge of the mountain, along which the Dudley Trail descends to the pond. To the southwest you'll see the Knife Edge, probably the most exciting nontechnical traverse in the East. Hikers are advised to terminate their climb at this spot if the weather turns bad.

To head over to Baxter Peak, bear left

The Knife Edge, seen from Baxter Peak

or southwest on the Knife Edge Trail and descend into a gully between Pamola and nearby Chimney Peak. Cairns and paint blazes mark the route. On your right you'll pass the Chimney, a steep cleft suitable only for technical climbers. You rise steeply to the summit of Chimney Peak. Beyond it, you are entirely in the open on the Knife as you move southwestward to the two highest summits on Katahdin.

The Knife Edge is a two- or three-foot wide path that drops off precipitously on both sides. On the east side, the ridge plunges quickly down to the Avalanche Brook drainage area and, on the other, toward the South Basin. High winds and clouds can make this a dangerous section of trail. You proceed over a series of knobs and arrive at the lowest point on the Knife in .5 mile. The trail then ascends the South Peak of Katahdin on steep grades, crossing the summit .8 mile from Pamola. In another .3 mile you'll arrive on Baxter Peak, Maine's highest summit and northern terminus of the Appalachian Trail.

The views from Baxter Peak are described in detail in Hike 35, which approaches Katahdin from the south side of the park. You may have noticed that, although the Knife Edge looks greenish gray overall, where foot traffic has worn a path the rocks are pink. For a brief geological explanation, see Hike 35's description of the rocks on Baxter Peak and on the Tableland. You may also be interested in the differences between the granite of Katahdin and that of its closest neighbor, described in Hike 32, South Turner Mountain.

From Baxter Peak, you could retrace your steps back over the Knife Edge and down; however, in less time you can complete a circuit and see new trails. The distance is a bit farther, but easier traveling will make up the time.

From the peak, descend gradually northwest on the Tableland, away from the Knife Edge and toward the Saddle, passing the Cathedral Trail, Baxter Peak Cutoff, and Cathedral Cutoff trails. (You can also take the Cathedral Trail down to Chimney Pond if there are no children or inexperienced hikers in your group. This book recommends the Saddle Trail down to Chimney Pond because it is easier and safer for someone who is already half worn out from the Knife Edge.) From Baxter Peak, the Saddle Trail leads in 2.2 miles to Chimney Pond.

After you have walked 1 mile down into the Saddle, you will be standing between Baxter and Hamlin peaks. The Saddle Trail turns right and drops off the Tableland down a fairly stationary rock slide for .2 mile. Be careful not to dislodge rocks onto people below; likewise, keep a defensive eye on people above. The slide came down in 1893, and in 1927 LeRoy Dudley opened the trail from Chimney Pond to the bottom of the slide.

Below the slide, the trail enters scrub growth, crosses a small brook, and descends more gradually through birch and spruce-fir woods, flattening out at the bottom of the Great Basin. The trail ends at the center of Chimney Pond Campground, where there are lean-tos and a bunkhouse available by prior reservation.

Chimney Pond is the campground's drinking water supply, and no washing or swimming is allowed here. In another twenty minutes, however, 1.3 miles down the trail to Roaring Brook, you'll be able to enjoy the cold glory of the Basin Ponds. Meanwhile, feast your eyes on picturesque Chimney Pond, with its large boulders fallen from the Knife Edge. The Great Basin is a cirque carved by a glacier that ground downward from the top of Katahdin. The Knife Edge was carved when glaciers grated down both its sides, leaving the slender arête or backbone standing. The glaciers pushed rock debris down the mountainside and left the bulldozed piles and walls, called moraines, when they melted. The Basin Ponds are dammed by such moraines. Chimney Pond is only six to eight feet deep and freezes to the bottom in winter, rendering it uninhabitable for fish.

You will descend the Chimney Pond Trail, which exits from behind the bunk-house, for 3.3 miles to Roaring Brook. At .6 mile, you'll pass on the left a depression called Dry Pond that holds water in spring or after a heavy rain and is rimmed by a glacial moraine. You'll cross several brooks, and at 1 mile you will pass the North Basin Cutoff, which leads in .7 mile to the North Basin Trail. At 1.3 miles you reach an open area near the shore of Basin Pond, an excel-

lent place for swimming. To the left along the shore is an old lumberman's dam at the outlet. The Basin Ponds are a string of three ponds along a glacial moraine; this one is the lowest of the three.

Beyond Basin Ponds the descent is more moderate, following an old lumbering road through a hardwood forest. At 2.2 miles from Chimney Pond, you cross a bridge over the outlet brook from Pamola Pond and then cross several smaller brooks. At 2.7 miles, you begin paralleling Roaring Brook, occasionally seeing pieces of old telephone wire that used to connect to the Chimney Pond ranger station. Finally, at 3.3 miles, you pass the Helon Taylor Trail (your earlier ascent) and the Russell Pond Trail and return to Roaring Brook Campground, where you sign in, having completed your 10-mile circuit of Katahdin.

Katahdin: Abol Slide & Hunt Trail

Total distance (round trip): 11 miles
Hiking time: 9 hours
Vertical rise: 3,980 feet
Maps: USGS 7.5' Mount Katahdin, Doubletop Mountain;
  USGS 15' Katahdin, Harrington Lake; Baxter Park Map;
  MATC 1 (1988)

The Abol Trail on Mount Katahdin provides a steep, direct ascent to Thoreau Spring on the Tableland and to Baxter Peak, Maine's highest summit. The spring, at 4,636 feet, is located at the junction of the Abol, Hunt (Appalachian), and Baxter Peak Cutoff trails. This route ascends the old Abol Slide, formed in 1816, and its outwash. The Abol Trail, probably the oldest regular route to the summit, is the second of two approaches to Katahdin's major peaks suggested in this book. The 11-mile circuit can be shortened by 2 miles (45 minutes) if you spot a car at Katahdin Stream Campground, 2 miles west of Abol Campground (trailhead). The only water available on the trail besides surface water is Thoreau Spring, which can almost dry up in summer. It is best to carry plenty of water with you.

To begin the climb, drive to Abol Campground, 6 miles northwest of the Togue Pond Gate on the Nesowadnehunk Road. From the trail signs at the northeast corner of Abol Campground, you depart northward as the trail ascends, following blue blazes to the south side of a feeder brook at about .2

mile. Evidence of moose is frequently seen in the hardwood forest and later in the spruce-fir forest. As the walk grows more steep, you proceed through tall, dense spruce forest, bearing northeast away from the brook at .8 mile from the campground. At just over 1 mile you cross a small brook where old logging roads intersect the trail.

Continuing northeast, you arrive on the gravelly terrain that marks the beginning of the slide outwash area at 1.3 miles. The outwash, once barren, is now covered with mixed growth, which gradually thins out as you ascend. The grade becomes increasingly steep in this section and ascends on gravel and loose scree. Use caution, as the footing is poor. Be careful, too, not to dislodge stones onto hikers below.

The slide is made up of many different rock types. Katahdin granite at this level is gray or white, but pink rocks from the top have been carried down here by water and ice. You may see some sedimentary rocks containing fossils, rocks much older than Katahdin itself. These are glacial "erratics" that were carried from the northwest by gla-

Lunch at Thoreau Spring on Katahdin's Tableland

ciers, bulldozed up and over Katahdin, and deposited on the south side. For a more thorough explanation of erratics, see Hike 40, Doubletop.

At just under 2 miles, the trail levels off briefly and then climbs up a more recent slide. Excellent views begin to open up to the south, but given the stiff angle of ascent, you'll need to focus your attention on your footing. Still climbing steeply, you'll crest the slide at 2.3 miles, moving onto the Tableland through a field of sharply angled boulders. The trail takes a more comfortable route across the plateau above the boulders, following blue blazes, arriving shortly at Thoreau Spring. In fair weather, this spot makes a good rest stop, given its excellent perspectives on the south and west.

If the weather is bad, head left on the Hunt Trail (also the Appalachian Trail) to descend. Otherwise, turn right or east

for the 1-mile trek to Baxter Peak. Follow the signs and white blazes for the Hunt (Appalachian) Trail to the summit. The climb is gradual here, nothing like the slide, and, in .3 mile, you move up over a ledgy section along the lip of the plateau. In this link between Thoreau Spring and Baxter Peak you are traversing the final portion of the Appalachian Trail, which ends on the summit. (Beginning on Springer Mountain in Georgia, the trail wends its way the full length of the Atlantic coast states over 2,100 miles to Katahdin. Nearly 280 miles of the Appalachian Trail lie in Maine.) A brief sprint above the Tableland brings you onto 5,267-foot Baxter Peak.

The actual climb in this last part of the hike is moderate, but the trail is extremely exposed. Don't get caught here in inclement weather. Climatic conditions on Katahdin rival those of Mount Washington in their severity. Storm systems can move in without warning in just minutes. Be prepared to head down.

The views from Baxter Peak are enough to shake up even the most jaded (if the scramble up the slides didn't do that for you already). Due north, across the majestic South and Great basins, are Katahdin's three northern peaks. To the southeast is South Peak connected, on its left, by the Knife Edge to Chimney Peak and Pamola. From here, you begin to get an idea of the mountain's massive size. Pack along a USGS 15′ Katahdin map. It will help you to identify the dozens of peaks that surround the Katahdin massif, trailing west and north toward Canada.

To the south, the many ponds in and outside the park lie like a shattered mirror, and behind them lies Nesowadnehunk Deadwater on the West Branch of the Penobscot. Southwest, Big and Little Spencer mountains (Hike 31) lie together behind Chesuncook Lake, with Big Squaw (Hike 28) in the distance.

At Baxter Peak and on the Tableland, you may have noticed that the rocks are a different color from those on the Abol Slide. All these rocks are Katahdin granite, but at higher elevations the granite is pink instead of white due to a higher potassium content in the granite's feldspar. Higher potassium levels were in the "melt" of the molten magma that welled up underground from deep inside the earth and formed the Katahdin granite pluton. More of the story can be read in Hike 40, Doubletop, and Hike 32, South Turner Mountain. Of course, the whole Tableland and Knife Edge look greenish gray because the rock surfaces are covered with lichen, but if you look at recently overturned rocks in the trails and where foot traffic has worn off the lichen, you will see that the actual granite is pink.

It is also curious that so many of the rocks here are broken to nearly the same size and shape. This is because granite has its own pattern of "jointing" or breaking at certain intervals and at specific angles. Although jointing size varies from location to location (compare with South Turner and other granite mountains), the jointing is locally uniform, and the angles are always consistent. Katahdin's Tableland thus looks like a field of uniform boulders.

To descend the mountain, retrace your steps 1 mile from Baxter Peak to Thoreau Spring. From here you can climb back down the Abol Slide; or, for a more scenic and exciting trip down, take the Hunt Spur (Appalachian Trail), a longer trail that leads to Katahdin Stream Campground, 2 miles from where you started at Abol Campground.

To descend via the Hunt Trail, cut by Irving Hunt in the 1890s, follow the white AT blazes west from Thoreau Spring across the Tableland. When you reach the "Gateway" at the edge of the Tableland, the trail literally drops off over the side, down a knife edge of the Hunt Spur for the first .2 mile. Views here are breathtaking, but stop walking when you want to gaze—the pathway here is narrow and dangerous, unforgiving if you should take a wrong step.

Witherle Ravine is the deep pit on your right, walled by the Owl (Hike 35). Beyond it are the Klondike and Fort mountains, with their "fir waves," peculiar stripes of downed trees, which have numerous hypothetical explanations of origin. You scramble steeply down huge boulders until the trail becomes less steep and dangerous at the 3849-foot elevation point, .5 mile below the Gateway. Here is the end of the Hunt Spur, and the Hunt Trail continues down through enormous boulders, some the size of a house. One year I climbed Katahdin on this trail with a full backpack on a five-day trip. Luckily, I met a minister and his two sons who helped me pass my pack up over some of these ledges and through the "lemon squeezes" along the way.

You enter woods 1.5 miles from the Gateway and shortly pass The Cave, a small slab cave that is the first possible shelter on your trip down. Nearly 1 mile into the trees you reach O-Joy Brook, so named by thirsty hikers who had found Thoreau Spring dry. The woods get prettier as you descend a ravine and begin to hear Katahdin Stream as it approaches the falls. About 2.5 miles from the Gateway, several side trails to the right take you to viewpoints of Katahdin Falls. Soon the trail passes close by the falls.

Katahdin Stream is usually spanned by a footbridge. If the bridge here is out of commission, though, keep walking to a crossing farther downstream. Pick your way across the stream, using a stick if necessary. As in all stream crossings, unbuckle your backpack before crossing so that, should you fall, you can extricate yourself quickly to avoid drowning.

You pass the trail to the Owl and then walk for 1 more mile through wonderfully level terrain and hardwoods to Katahdin Stream Campground. Your trip now ends if you have left a car here. If not, head east (left) on the park road for 2 miles to Abol Campground and your car.

35

The Owl

Total distance (round trip): 6.6 miles
Hiking time: 5 hours
Vertical rise: 2,630 feet
Maps: USGS 7.5′ Mount Katahdin, Doubletop Mountain;
  USGS 15′ Katahdin, Harrington Lake; Baxter Park Map

The Owl rises, rather like an observation post, in the midst of Baxter and close to Katahdin, just west of Baxter Peak. The structure is actually a granite knob severed from Katahdin by Katahdin Stream. From the Owl, you can look north to North Brother, Fort, and Mullen mountains. These peaks lie beyond Klondike Pond and the great boggy area known as the Klondike. The Klondike, itself, forms a kind of catch basin for all water runoff from Coe, O-J-I, and Barren mountains, the Owl, and the western arms of Katahdin. It's ideal moose territory. To the east lies Witherle Ravine. Baxter and Hamlin peaks tower more than a thousand feet above. The Owl also affords a fine outlook onto the ponds to the southwest.

The route to the Owl begins on the Hunt Trail (Appalachian Trail) at Katahdin Stream Campground, on the Park Perimeter Road, midway between Nesowadnehunk Campground and Togue Pond gatehouses. Water should be carried. Although the Hunt Trail had once been relocated to the south side of Katahdin Stream to decrease wear on

View of the Owl from Hunt Trail on Katahdin

an eroded section, the trail has been re-located yet again and follows the stream's *north* side once more. You will travel north and northeast along the stream, following white (AT) blazes.

Continue northeast on easy grades to just over 1 mile, where the Owl Trail bears left onto a blue-blazed trail, as the Hunt Trail runs nearly due east. You ascend more rapidly, and cross a stream .5 mile above the trail junction, 1.6 miles from the trailhead.

After a relatively easy half mile, you begin a steep ascent into a shallow ravine and out onto an old slide. At 3.1 miles, a side trail will take you a few feet away to a cliff overlooking Katahdin, with the Hunt Spur (AT) rising on its southwest flank. The main trail then climbs more steeply through dense scrub spruce to the upper ledges, past a balancing rock. You see views of the Owl's conelike summit at 3.2 miles. A short walk on less steep, grassy terrain brings you to the top at 3.3 miles.

Standing on the Owl's summit, you are on the lower right section of an L shaped formation of mountains called "the Katahdinauogh" by Indians. Stretching northwest and then northeast, other peaks in the L include: Barren, Mount O-J-I (Hike 38), Mount Coe, South and North Brother (Hike 39), and Fort and Mullen mountains.

Two waterfalls in Witherle Ravine may be seen if you walk 50 yards through scrub growth along the ridge. Above, to the east, rise Katahdin's highest peaks. Henry David Thoreau climbed to the summits near here on his first trip up the Penobscot in September, 1846. His words, even now, capture the wild, lonely spirit of the great expanse of Katahdin and its surrounding mountains: ". . . I climbed alone over huge rocks, loosely poised, a mile or more, still edging toward the clouds; for though the

day was clear elsewhere, the summit was concealed by mist. The mountain seemed a vast aggregation of loose rocks, as if some time it had rained rocks, and they lay as they fell on the mountainsides, no where fairly at rest, but leaning on each other, all rocking stones, with cavities between, but scarcely any soil or smoother shelf. They were the raw materials of a planet dropped from an unseen quarry, which the vast chemistry of nature would anon work up, or work down, into the smiling and verdant plants and valleys of earth. This was an undone extremity of the globe."

Like the other mountains surrounding Katahdin, the Owl was once part of the same granite mass as Katahdin, long before the mass was cracked, weathered, and carved down into separate smaller mountains. More detailed descriptions of this process can be found in Hike 32, South Turner Mountain, Hikes 33 and 34 of Katahdin, and Hike 40, Doubletop.

Use the same trail on the trek down.

36

Niagara Falls

Total distance: 2.5 miles
Hiking time: 1½ hours
Vertical rise: none
Maps: USGS 7.5' Doubletop Mountain, Rainbow Lake East;
  USGS 15' Harrington Lake; Baxter Park Map; MATC 1
  (1988)

Big Niagara and Little Niagara Falls are within minutes of each other on Nesowadnehunk Stream at the south end of Baxter State Park. Both sets of falls are dramatic and, along with Toll Dam, offer some interesting stops on your hike.

The hike to Niagara Falls begins at Daicey Pond. Follow the Nesowadnehunk Tote Road 10.7 miles from the Togue Pond entry gate to the turnoff (sign) for Daicey Pond Camps, and drive 1.4 miles to the camps, where you park. (If you are staying in a cabin, you

Little Niagara Falls

may park in the cabin parking area; otherwise park in the field to the right of the road, just before you get to the pond.)

Look for the Appalachian Trail (AT) sign and follow the trail's white blazes south away from the pond and camps, toward Nesowadnehunk Stream. The path is often wet and muddy.

When the trail curves west (right), you can see Nesowadnehunk Stream to your right through the raspberries and alders. Continue through dense spruce and long beech fern. In early spring you can also see Canada mayflower, chickweed, trailing arbutus, and wild oats. You pass near an alder-choked deadwater beside the stream into an opening. To the right lie the ruins of a cabin; and Squaw's Bosom and Doubletop outline the background. A few more yards on the left, another cabin stands in ruins.

Shortly, a side trail on the right takes you 100 feet through raspberries and alders to Toll Dam, which has had three lives in the lumbering history of the Nesowadnehunk. The high wooden supports still standing are part of the original dam, built in the 1850s without a spike—it was put together entirely with hardwood pegs, still visible. This was also one of the first sites in the country to be dynamited. The stagecoach company refused to haul the dynamite, and it was finally carried to the dam site by horse and bateau. The dam was abandoned when its operators went out of business for charging exorbitant rates for log driving.

The dam was rebuilt twice more, the last time by the Great Northern Paper Company in 1929. The two ruined camps you passed earlier were part of this operation—the one on your right was the kitchen and main quarters of the crew who built the dam and later of the crew who drove the logs. The cabin on your left was an office and later a tractor shed.

Just after you return to the main trail from Toll Dam, another short side trail leads you to the right to Little Niagara Falls, where you can stand on a giant boulder and watch the stream froth and pitch below you. Upstream is Toll Dam with Mount O-J-I (Hike 38) and the cap of Mount Coe in the background.

Return to the AT and walk another .3 mile (passing a spring 60 feet off the trail on your left) to a side trail on the right that takes off steeply downhill to Big Niagara Falls. Here you can pick your way out onto rocks in the stream for a trout's-eye view of the falls.

The rock of Big and Little Niagara Falls is Katahdin granite, part of the vast mass of rock that included Katahdin, Turner, Doubletop, and surrounding mountains in one huge pluton (an underground mass of rock that was intruded as molten magma). Nesowadnehunk Stream has cut down through the granite at the falls, exposing impressive sections of granite with its flashy flecks of mica, white chunks of feldspar, and transparent jewels of quartz.

Here and there you can see where the granite, which is easily cracked or "jointed" by weathering conditions, was cleaved and the cracks later filled with different rock intruding up from the earth's mantle. Katahdin granite, the youngest rock unit in Baxter Park, is approximately 360 million years old, and the crack fillings or "dikes" have formed since that time.

When you've had your fill of falls, scramble back up the steep bank, turn left onto the AT, and follow the white blazes back to Daicey Pond.

37

Sentinel Mountain

Total distance: 5.8 miles
Hiking time: 4 hours
Vertical rise: 1,100 feet
Maps: USGS 7.5' Doubletop Mountain, Rainbow Lake East;
*   USGS 15' Harrington Lake; Baxter Park Map*

Sentinel Mountain is truly the sentinel of the southwestern corner of Baxter State Park. Its summit affords dramatic views north to Mount Katahdin, Doubletop, and the Cross Range, and south outside the park to Rainbow Lake and distant mountains on the Appalachian Trail.

To reach the trailhead, drive Baxter Park's Nesowadnehunk Tote Road (Park Perimeter Road) from the Togue Pond Gate west to Foster Field and turn south at the sign to Kidney Pond Camps, where you will park.

The trail runs west from the library and goes behind the cabins. Beyond the last cabin a trail sign indicates where the blue blazes for the trail begin. Skirt the shore .2 mile to Jackson Landing. Canada mayflower is abundant along the trail, as is clintonia lily, named for Governor Dewitt Clinton of New York. It is also called yellow bead lily. Its two to three distinct lily leaves encircle one stem bearing yellow blossoms in spring and inedible blue beads in late summer and fall. Also noticeable around Kidney Pond are numerous grackles and the sweet song of the white-throated sparrow.

At Jackson Landing, a trail leads right to Jackson and Celia ponds, but you continue skirting the pond another .2 mile to the next junction. Here you leave Kidney Pond Trail and turn right (west) on the trail to Sentinel Mountain, the summit of which is 2.2 miles from this turn. The trail ascends, gradually at first, through birch and spruce, blackberries, painted trillium, and purple wake-robin in early spring. In summer the wood sorrel and spinulose wood fern are more evident. As the trail rises, the spruce get taller. The trail clears a ridge, where I once came face-to-face with a bull moose, and then descends the ridge through violets, chickweed, and trillium to a log bridge over Sentinel Mountain Brook. Across the brook the trail rises gradually southwest through spruce and birch, crosses a bog of cedars and sphagnum moss, and then opens into sheep laurel, bunchberry, and wintergreen. You cross a log into a green setting of fallen trees and rocks carpeted with moss.

Keep walking southwest through mixed woods, more open because the trees are larger and therefore less numerous. The trail crosses Sentinel Brook again and follows it a short way before crossing again near a huge boulder cave. Here the trail becomes steep, still following the stream bed through clintonia lily, trillium, and rosy twisted-stalk. Long beech fern grows on the rocks in the dry stream bed.

You cross and recross the stream bed, and then leave it and rise into a notch between the east and west summits of Sentinel Mountain. The west peak to the right is the more interesting with its loop trail around the summit. Climb boulders to the top and begin the summit loop clockwise, looking south across the West Branch of the Penobscot and Rainbow Lake to distant mountains on the Appalachian Trail. As you circle through blueberries and reindeer lichen you may see a red-eyed spruce grouse. At the far end of the loop, "Parson's Pulpit" offers a dramatic view north to Squaw's Bosom, Doubletop (Hike 40), O-J-I (Hike 38), with the cap of Mount Coe behind, Barren, and Katahdin (Hikes 33–34). Completing the loop, you have a good view down between Sentinel and Katahdin of Lily Pad Pond, shaped startlingly like a lily pad, complete with stem.

At the end of the summit loop, retrace the trail back to Kidney Pond.

38

Mount O-J-I

Total distance: 6.4 miles
Hiking time: 5½ hours
Vertical rise: 2,340 feet
Maps: USGS 7.5' Doubletop Mountain; USGS 15' Harrington
  Lake; Baxter Park Map

Rising north of the Nesowadnehunk Valley in the southwestern area of Baxter State Park is Mount O-J-I, named for the three slides on its southwest face that at one time resembled these letters. A storm in September 1932 caused more slides, changing the letter configuration. Today, the *J* resembles an ostrich. A new slide in 1954 southeast of the *I* slide forms the South Slide Trail and provides a circuit route from the North Slide Trail, which is part of the former letter *O*. The loop trail ascends the North Slide Trail, runs the ridge, and descends the South Slide Trail.

The O-J-I hike begins at the Nesowadnehunk Tote Road (Park Perimeter Road) at a point 10.9 miles west of the Togue Pond Gate (the southeastern entrance to Baxter Park), across the road from Foster Field (sign) and the turn for Kidney Pond Camps. Park in Foster Field and follow the blue-blazed trail north into the woods, passing first a small brook on your left and then cutting through a cedar swamp. At .4 mile, take the left fork to the North Slide Trail. You will return to this junction from the South Slide Trail (right fork).

On the North Slide Trail, you cross another brook and walk through a blow-down area that is gradually recovering from a storm in the fall of 1974. At .7 mile, you cross a brook and ascend gradually through maturing hardwoods and many wildflowers on the forest floor: spring beauty, Canada mayflower, and trillium in May; bunchberry, Indian pipe, and wood sorrel in summer; asters and the berries of Canada mayflower (red), trillium (red), clintonia (blue), and bunchberry (red) in fall.

At 1.3 miles, you cross a brook in an open gravel wash formed by the slide. From here, the trail ascends more steeply; at 1.7 miles it bears right and follows a rocky stream bed at the bottom of the north slide. Soon you cross smooth, steeply sloping granite ledges, which are treacherous in wet weather. The slide opens to a 75-yard width, curves to the northeast, and skirts left of an insurmountable smooth cliff, following steep ledges up. At 2.5 miles, the trail bears right through scrub birch and ascends steeply on rotten gravel. Shortly you reach the head of the slide and enter the woods, where a 50-yard walk allows you to crest the ridge. At the crest, a side trail leads .4 mile left to Old Jay

Eye Rock (mileage not included), a choice lookout over the Nesowadnehunk Valley.

At 2.7 miles, you reach the first open peak of O-J-I, looking north to Mount Coe and northwest up the Nesowadnehunk Valley. Better views are from the second peak, 50 yards beyond the first (3,410 feet). To the southeast you have a close-up of Barren Mountain, an unadvisable bushwhack away. Farther east is an impressive view of the west side of Katahdin. Just below you, look east into the Klondike Bowl, which holds Klondike

Pond, one of the highest ponds in Maine at 3,400 feet. The Klondike is one of two spots in Baxter Park too impractical ever to be logged. (The other is up the side of The Traveler from Howe Brook, see Hikes 44 and 45.) Few people have entered the dark, dense, swampy Klondike, and I understand that even fewer have returned to tell about it.

In 1963 a herd of Newfoundland caribou was transported by helicopter to the northwest plateau of Katahdin with the hope of establishing a permanent herd. The adults, however, with migra-

Mount O-J-I behind Little Niagara Falls and Toll Dam

tion patterns imprinted in Newfoundland, left the mountain never to return. Since then there have been two possible sightings of a caribou, in 1975 and 1979. Twenty-six years later, in 1989, another herd of Caribou was set free in Baxter Park, twelve adults initially, with plans to add to the herd periodically to build it to a hundred animals. It will be interesting to trace the progress of this incipient herd.

Following blue blazes, leave the summit of O-J-I and descend the ridge for .1 mile, passing on your right a short side trail to Kidney Pond Lookout, with open views southwest and a topside view of the J slide below. At .2 mile you pass the junction with the O-J-I link (which leads left half a mile to the Mt. Coe Trail). The trail then drops below the ridge another .2 mile to the head of the south slide. The next .5 mile is steep and tedious going, but 1 mile from the summit, the trail descends more moderately over loose outwash from the slide and into the woods.

When you have gone 1.6 miles from the summit, you descend gradually through mature beech forest and walk back through the 1974 blowdown to the junction with the North Slide Trail at 2.5 miles. Another .4 mile returns you to the road at Foster Field.

North Brother Mountain

Total distance (round trip); 8 miles
Hiking time: 7 hours
Vertical rise: 2,935 feet
Maps: USGS 7.5' Doubletop Mountain, Mount Katahdin;
  USGS 15' Harrington Lake, Katahdin; Baxter Park Map

The Brothers, rising southeast of the Cross Range, provide a strenuous hike from the Nesowadnehunk Road that culminates in excellent outlooks over the Klondike, the Northwest Basin and Plateau, and the Howe Peaks of Katahdin. The trail runs from Slide Dam to North Brother Mountain over the north-

Bear track

west shoulder of South Brother. A rough side trail also takes in the summit of South Brother.

The Marston Trail, constructed in the mid-1950s by Philip and James Marston, begins at Slide Dam on the park service road about 6 miles north of Katahdin Stream Ranger Station and about 2.8 miles south of Nesowadnehunk (Sourdnahunk) Field Campground. Park off the road here. Leaving the east side of the road opposite the Slide Dam picnicking area, you head eastward along the blue-blazed Marston Trail on the north side of Slide Brook. In a short while you bear left, climbing through a forested area to the south of another brook. Ascending briskly, the path stays with this brook, crossing and recrossing the waterway several times.

At 1.2 miles, passing through stands of mixed hardwoods and conifers, you cross the brook once again and arrive at a stone cairn. The Mount Coe Trail departs to the right here. Continue along the Marston Trail, cross Roaring Brook at 1.4 miles, and ascend steadily into a bowl between South Brother and the Cross Range. The trail begins an increasingly steep march, up the south slope of the Cross Range, with occasional views to Doubletop Mountain to the west.

The top of the climb is crested at 2.5 miles, where you plunge back into spruce and fir woods and into a sag between North and South Brother. At 3.1 miles, the South Brother Side Trail is passed on your right. A cairn marks the junction. There are good views from this summit, and you may want to add 1.6 miles (round trip) to your hike and make the side trip to South Brother (3,942 feet elevation). The Marston Trail runs northeast from this junction along the north buttress of South Brother, and then descends into the cleft between it and North Brother. The steep climb resumes. At 3.7 miles, you emerge from scrub woodland and begin the final ascent above timberline through a boulder-strewn area, arriving on the summit after a few minutes climb, 4 miles above your starting point.

The summit of North Brother (4,143 feet) makes a first-class observation point for the western area of Baxter. Hamlin Peak and the Howe Peaks of Katahdin are to the immediate southeast. Russell Mountain is to the northeast; Mullen Mountain to the north. The Cross Range strikes out to the northwest and of course, Doubletop (Hike 40) makes an imposing sight to the west. One of the virtues of the long hike to the top of North Brother is the feeling of wildness, of isolation that comes only in country where so little human evidence is visible.

Retrace your steps to reach Slide Dam. Watch the trail carefully; it is sometimes hard to follow in poor weather conditions. Just in case the occasion arises, forget any ideas of communing with the larger wildlife up close; moose have minds of their own.

(If you hike the South Brother Side Trail on this route, add about 1.6 miles to the total distance and an additional half-hour walking time.)

Doubletop Mountain

Total distance (round trip): 6.6 miles
Hiking time: 5 hours
Vertical rise: 2,450 feet
Maps: USGS 7.5' Doubletop Mountain; USGS 15' Harrington
  Lake; Baxter Park Map

The trek up this mountain leads to excellent views of many of the western
peaks in Baxter State Park, particularly
to the west flanks of Katahdin and
southwest to the low, wild hills along the
West Branch of the Penobscot. Doubletop's east side plunges sharply down to
the Nesowadnehunk Valley in ripples of
bright, weathered rock, making a striking sight from the road. With the opening of a new trail from the north in 1969
and 1970, the trail from the south (not
described here) became less traveled. It
is now possible to make a complete traverse of the mountain, though, from
Nesowadnehunk Field in the north to
Kidney Pond in the south. The trail described here takes you from the north
side to the two peaks, returning round
trip to the north where you parked at
Nesowadnehunk Field and Campground.

Many hundreds of acres in southwest
Baxter Park were damaged by high
winds in 1974. This blowdown was especially destructive on the slopes of
Doubletop. You will see the young forest
recovering from the devastation.

The path in to Doubletop begins at
Nesowadnehunk Campground, 16.8

miles from the Togue Pond gate. You
can park at the campground parking lot
and walk to the last tent site on
Nesowadnehunk Stream, where a sign
marks the trail to Doubletop. It is 3.1
miles to the 3488-foot north peak and
3.3 miles to the slightly lower south
peak.

You are hiking the favorite trail, in all
of Baxter Park, of the late Gerald Merry,
former park naturalist. He loved this trail
for its woodland splendor—its many
species of ferns and wildflowers and its
tremendous yellow (silver) birches and
maples.

The trail lies near Nesowadnehunk
Stream, which you can often hear, and
crosses its tributaries from time to time,
staying fairly level for the first 1.2 miles
to Doubletop Brook. The woods are
spruce-fir mixed with abundant mature
hardwoods. The forest floor, rich in leaf
litter, is typical of a hardwood forest, fes-
tooned with fern species (spinulose
woodfern, interrupted, oak, and long
beech fern) and dainty wildflowers such
as rosy twisted-stalk, clintonia lily, violets, Canada mayflower, painted trillium,
hobblebush, oxalis (wood sorrel), and
ladyslipper. From time to time, Indian

Williams
Pond

Nesowadnehunk
Field

Ranger
GATE Sta.

Nesowadnehunk Field
Campground

CAMPGROUND

NESOWADNEHUNK

Ledge
Falls

PICNIC AREA

STREAM

Slide
Dam

Picnic Area

N

Mount   Veto

Squaws

Doubletop
Mountain

0   0.5   1.0 mile

cucumber root is abundant along the trail.

At 1.2 miles, the trail crosses Doubletop Brook on a footbridge and shoots steeply up a raw, eroded slope denuded by the 1974 blowdown. The woods will be recovering from this storm for a long time. Rotting trunks and exposed roots bear witness to the damage this windstorm caused. One consolation is the views to your right (west) of Mount Veto, not visible before the blowdown. The trail shows frequent sign of moose, and for about a mile, it is excruciatingly steep.

An unusual rock lies in the trail here— a two-foot rounded hunk of white limestone covered with fossil imprints of brachiopods.

Just when you can take the steep grade no longer, the trail eases and nearly levels out on a comfortable plateau forested with a wonderland of wildflowers, sphagnum moss, and dwarfed trees. The haunting pull of this glen might have made this the naturalist's favorite section, and it is a lovely flat walk that allows you to rest before the final steep, but short, ascent of the 3488-foot north peak. From the peak, excellent views spread in all directions, although the firetower has been toppled to avoid liability. Below you lie Ledge Falls, Nesowadnehunk Field, and Nesowadnehunk Lake, "Sowdyhunk" in local parlance. To your right (east), Mount O-J-I rises with its three slides, Mount Coe lies close beside it, and South Brother rests in front of North Brother. The Cross Range is slightly to the left. Over O-J-I is the regal outline of Katahdin, from Hamlin Peak in the north to Baxter Peak in the south behind the Owl. To the west, Mount Veto is bisected by the park's western boundary, which continues south to Squaw's Bosom. A short side trail to the east takes

you to a plaque mounted in a granite slab, a monument to Keppele Hall whose ashes were given to the winds on Doubletop in 1926.

From the north peak, it is a .2-mile walk to the south peak where the view of lakes and ponds is spectacular. To the west, the big lakes are first Harrington, then Ripogenus and Chesuncook, with Rainbow Lake in the distance beyond the West Branch of the Penobscot and Nesowadnehunk Deadwater. South of you, like a shattered mirror, lie more than a dozen ponds, including Slaughter, Rocky, Kidney, Jackson, Lily Pad, Daicey, Elbow, Grassy, and Lost ponds.

From here it is 4 miles south to the Kidney Pond Camps road, on an even steeper and less scenic trail down. I suggest retracing your steps the 3.3 miles over the north peak and down the naturalist's favorite trail to Nesowadnehunk Field Campground.

As you descend and again pass the limestone rock with brachiopod fossils, you might wonder where it came from and how it got there. The answer is a long story. A shallow ocean covered eastern North America, including all of Maine, for 200 million years in the early Paleozoic Era, during which time layers of sediment eroded from the continent, washed into the ocean, and accumulated in layers. Ancient marine organisms, like these brachiopods, lived and died in the layers of sediment, which gradually hardened and turned to sandstone, shale, and limestone. Since that time, volcanoes erupted about 400 million years ago from the ancient sea, creating the Traveler rhyolite seen in Hikes 41–45. Then, 360 million years ago, the Katahdin granite was formed as a huge underground "blister" of molten rock that welled up, cooled, and hardened over millions of years. Doubletop is a frag-

Doubletop from Baxter Park Road

ment of the huge buried Katahdin granite mass, which was gradually exposed by erosion and shattered by weathering into the many fragmentary pieces visible today—the Cross Range, the Brothers, Mount Coe, Doubletop, the Owl, South Turner, Katahdin, and others.

In the last million years, glaciers have periodically covered Maine and much of North America, moving loads of rock, gravel, sand, and clay from northwest to southeast. Pieces of many different kinds of rock were broken off, "entrained" by the glaciers, and carried

south. The fossil limestone on Doubletop is an "erratic," a rock from another location transported here probably 25,000 years ago by a glacier. It probably came an unknown distance from sedimentary rock that formed under the ocean long before the Katahdin granite welled up from inside the earth. If you look carefully, you can find other fossiliferous rocks under uprooted trees and along streams. Note, however, that rocks are protected, just as plants and animals, in Baxter State Park. They may not be collected or taken from the park.

41

Horse Mountain

Total distance: 2.8 miles
Hiking time: 1½ hours
Vertical rise: 800 feet
Maps: USGS 7.5' Trout Brook Mountain; USGS 15' Traveler
  Mountain; Baxter Park Map

Horse Mountain, formerly Matagamon Mountain, stands guardian over the Matagamon Gate entrance in the northeast corner of Baxter State Park. An abandoned Maine Forest Service (MFS) firetower on the summit offers outstanding views of Grand Lake Matagamon and The Traveler (Hikes 43 and 44) for only a little effort.

The trailhead is .6 mile west of the Matagamon Gate, which is 27 miles

Horse Mountain tower

northwest of Patten. As you drive into the park from the gate, you can see the sheer cliffs of Horse Mountain hanging over the road on your left. (Some technical rock climbing is done here, but not on the Horse Mountain hike.) Park on the left side of the Park Perimeter Road at the trailhead sign. There is no reliable water on this hike.

Follow the blue blazes south on the old tote road through mature mixed hardwoods. At .5 mile you pass large boulders and come shortly to a curve where an area of young second growth on the left marks a former woodyard. At one time a birch blight swept through this area, and the woodyard was part of logging operations that removed fallen trees before they rotted. On the ground bloom Canada mayflower, violets, and bunchberry in spring; bracken fern, wild sarsaparilla, sheep laurel, yarrow, hawkweed, and self-heal in summer; and jewelweed, blueberries, blackberries, and asters in late summer and fall.

Ascend moderately through maple and birch, past the fire watchman's five-foot-square emergency shelter. The trail steepens beyond the shelter and soon ends in dwarfed beech and birch at the open summit. You will follow the same trail back to your car.

Southwest from the tower hulk the massive peaks of The Traveler, at one time believed to be the second highest mountain in Maine. At the base of The Traveler, from left to right, lie Billfish Pond, Round Pond, Long and High ponds, and Littlefield Pond. Close by to the south is Billfish Mountain and west is Trout Brook Mountain. Spreading northwest to northeast is Grand Lake Matagamon. (Second Lake lies left of First Lake Matagamon.) To the southeast the East Branch of the Penobscot leaves Grand Lake Matagamon for Medway, where it joins the West Branch and heads for Bangor.

The parallel range that begins with Horse Mountain and extends south to Billfish Mountain and west to Trout Brook and Bald mountains was named the Deadwater Mountains by canoeists and lumbermen who came up the turbulent East Branch of the Penobscot and encountered the flat water of Grand Lake Matagamon. These mountains were in sight when the flat water was reached. The Deadwater Mountains were formed differently from the mountains further south. Whereas Katahdin and its satellites are granite, The Traveler and Deadwater Mountains are volcanic rhyolite, a tan rock of finer grain than granite. Both rhyolite and granite are formed of light minerals, silicates: sodium plagioclase feldspar, muscovite mica, quartz, and potassium feldspar. The only difference is the process of formation. Granite is intrusive (formed underground), and rhyolite is extrusive (volcanic).

Traveler rhyolite was formed as a volcano in a shallow sea about 400 million years ago. Katahdin granite was intruded underground like an enormous blister about 360 million years ago. Both rock types rose to much higher elevations when formed and have eroded

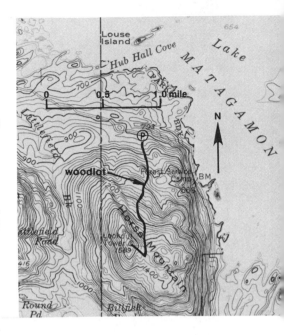

down to the current formations, only a fraction of their former height.

The summits of most of these mountains are bare or sparsely wooded, a result of the intense Great Wassataquoik Fire of 1903, which swept these mountains before funneling south through Pogy Notch into the Russell Pond area (Hike 50). The fire consumed even the topsoil, and now, eighty-five years later, the process of rebuilding the humus is only beginning. Hundreds of years will pass before soils can support normal growth.

An unsolved mystery goes with Billfish Pond. A pair of rusted boxcar wheels lies at the edge of the pond, and another pair is said to lie at its bottom. No one seems to know how they got there. There was never a railroad in the vicinity; the closest was the Eagle Lake and Umbazookis Railroad on the north end of Chamberlain Lake, thirty miles away.

South Branch Mountain

Total distance (around loop): 6 miles
Hiking time: 4½ hours
Vertical rise: 1,600 feet
Maps: USGS 7.5' Wassataquoik Lake; USGS 15' Traveler
  Mountain*; Baxter Park Map

The best views of The Traveler (Hikes 43 and 44) and Pogy Notch are seen from the ledges of South Branch Mountain. First blazed in 1964, the South Branch Mountain Trail provides a fine circuit over the mountain, around the ponds, and back to South Branch Campground. This route makes an excellent climb in conjunction with the hikes up The Traveler and Howe Brook. Good camping facilities, some interesting fishing possibilities, and a place to leave your car are all to be found along the shore of the ponds, and don't be surprised if you wake up to the sound of moose wading in the shallows at dawn.

Water should be carried on this hike. The trail commences at the west side of the campground near the northwest shore of Lower South Branch Pond. The pond outlet stream must be forded and is shallow. The trail runs southwest from the stream, shortly paralleling another brook for about .2 mile. Climbing on

comfortable grades, you ascend a ridgeline, bearing hard to the left and south at .8 mile above the trailhead.

Continuing southward, you shortly reach bare ledges that overlook the ponds and across to North Traveler. The trail runs along the side of the ridge, over a knob and across more ledge, allowing good views back toward the north end of the lower pond. The north summit of the mountain comes into sight in minutes as the trail pulls more to the right on steady grades. You top the North Peak at 2 miles, where views to the south begin to open up. The elevation of the North Peak is 2,599 feet.

Continuing southward, you drop into a slump briefly, then climb again to a trail junction where, at 2.5 miles from the campground, a short side trail leads right to the grassy, open south peak of South Branch Mountain, elevation 2,585 feet. One can see in all directions here, especially over the Deadwater Range, which runs toward the right to Nesowadnehunk Lake. Black Cat and Black Brook, Squirt Dam, Burnt, McCarty, Morse, and (more to the south) Strickland mountains form a staggered line southwest.

---

*Note: On the 15' USGS map for this area South Branch Mountain is referred to as Black Cat Mountain. The latter name is now associated with the east peak of Black Brook Mountain.

To the east, the ponds are below, and behind them rests the great hulk of The Traveler. To the southeast you can pick out North Turner Mountain and, further down to the right, Katahdin. Due northwest lies the wild, remote country Thoreau traversed by canoe over a hundred years ago and then wrote about in *The Maine Woods*.

From South Peak the trail continues down the south ridge through open meadows on easy grades. At the end of the meadows, at some rock outcrops, the trail turns left into a hardwood forest, descending steadily. There are some short, steep sections here. The angle of descent becomes more comfortable 1 mile below the summit as you follow a brook, continuing eastward. At 4.3 miles, a side trail leads 200 feet to Up-

per South Branch Pond lean-to, a quiet place to stay if you have made advance reservations with the Baxter State Park office (see introduction to this section). A network of brooks that feed Upper South Branch Pond is crossed soon in a boggy area grown up with alder scrub and marsh grass.

There are several attractive spots along the upper pond to stop and rest. On your way again, continue walking east to a junction with the Pogy Notch Trail at a wilderness campsite. Here you swing north and left along the east shore of the pond. The walk here is nearly level for about 2 miles back to the campground, with pleasant views over the water most of the way. Chances of spotting wildlife as you walk this section are very good.

North Traveler Mountain

Total distance (round trip): 5¼ miles
Hiking time: 5 hours
Vertical rise: 2,150 feet
Maps: USGS 7.5' Wassataquoik Lake, The Traveler; USGS 15'
 Traveler Mountain; Baxter Park Map

The Traveler is a rangy mountain mass running roughly north and south at the northern limits of Baxter State Park. This great mountain rises below First Grand Lake and close by the South Branch ponds. The mountain, with its five prominent summits, forms the eastern border of Pogy Notch. Burned over in 1903, the mountain is characterized by bald, open summits and high meadows, while the lower slopes show resurgent hardwood growth.

North Traveler is the only peak of the Traveler range, with the exception of the Peak of the Ridges (Hike 44), with a regular, clear trail. The route was originally cut by Myrle Scott, a Baxter ranger, and is probably the most used of the trails on the mountain.

The trail is approached on the park access road either from the south (if you're already in Baxter) or from the northeast via Patten. From Patten, take ME 159 west to Shin Pond, then follow a service road to the park. You turn left at "The Crossing" 33.5 miles west of Patten and bear south to South Branch Ponds Campground. The campground is 1.8 miles in from The Crossing and provides camping in a very attractive setting plus adequate parking for hikers'

cars. This area makes a convenient base for four of the five day hikes in the north end of the park covered in this book.

To head up North Traveler, you follow the Pogy Notch Trail from the east side of the campground. This first section of the trail arches around the north end of the northernmost of the two South Branch ponds. You shortly arrive at a trail junction and bear left onto the North Traveler Trail, commencing a brisk climb. At .5 mile from the campground, you move gradually out of deciduous forest, walking in a southeasterly direction along open ledges up the mountain's north ridge.

At just under 1 mile, you will pass a series of cliffs and walk under a knob, the trail leveling off slightly. The crest of the North Ridge is reached in a few minutes at another knob and, for nearly a half mile, you have level walking in the open. At 1.8 miles from the campground, you walk through more scrub growth, climbing again to the southeast. Watch for a short side trail on the left to a spring, which is the last reliable water on this route.

You see frequent signs of moose as the trail runs through a cluster of grassy uplands, dotted with ledges, for the next .5 mile. At 2.3 miles you re-enter the woods, climbing again through balsam and red spruce. You arrive on the open, ledgy summit of North Traveler in a few more minutes. The trail ends here.

The views from this spot are fine, covering as they do much of the wild lands to the north, west, and east of the park. To the east lie the headwaters of the East Branch of the Penobscot, while to the northeast you'll see Bald and Billfish mountains. Barrell Ridge is the low summit immediately to your north. Over the ridge, about six miles to the north-

northeast, is Trout Brook Mountain and, behind it, First Grand Lake.

You may have noticed the uniform color and consistency of the rock on North Traveler. This rock is Traveler rhyolite, left from 400 million years ago when a volcano erupted here in a shallow sea. The ancient volcano was much higher in elevation, and The Traveler with its starfish-shaped arms is merely its roots, exposed after millions of years of erosion.

You may see signs of a rough path leading to the south toward the other peaks on The Traveler range. This trip is trailless and is not recommended for any but the most experienced, fully equipped hiking party. The distance to the main summit of The Traveler and the return is four miles, and the route consists of a difficult bushwhack its entire length.

To regain the ponds, retrace your steps on the North Traveler Trail.

Rhyolite cliffs of the North Traveler

The Traveler — Peak of the Ridges

Total distance: 7.2 miles
Hiking time: 7 hours
Vertical rise: 2,240 feet
Maps: USGS 7.5' Wassataquoik Lake, The Traveler; USGS 15'
 Traveler Mountain; Baxter Park Map

The Traveler, once believed to be the second highest mountain in the state, presides over the northern end of Baxter State Park. The main summit is trailless, but approaches may be made to two lower peaks on the mountain. The higher of the two is Peak of the Ridges, where this hike will take you.

The Traveler was named by voyageurs who traveled the waterways of Maine and Canada trapping and logging. The large bulk and many radiating ridges of the mountain created the impression that the mountain moved or traveled along beside them.

The hike begins at South Branch Pond Campground, 2.3 miles down South Branch Pond Road, which leaves the Park Perimeter Road at a point 7 miles west of Matagamon Gate and 36 miles north of Togue Pond Gate.

From the campground you take off southeast on the Pogy Notch Trail, skirting Lower South Branch Pond. At .1 mile you pass the North Traveler Peak Trail on your left. The trail passes under the sheer North Ridge and brings you onto the delta of Howe Brook that separates Upper and Lower South Branch ponds. The two ponds used to be one

until they were divided by this delta.

The trail turns left and parallels the left bank of Howe Brook. At the trail junction 1 mile from the campground, take the right-hand path, staying on the Pogy Notch Trail. (The way left is the Howe Brook Trail, Hike 45.) The Pogy Notch Trail crosses and then leaves the brook to continue .3 mile across the flat delta through maturing white birches. You then scramble up a steep slope to the top of sheer cliffs, which drop into Upper South Branch Pond. At 1.5 miles, at the high point on the cliffs, is a trail junction. Ahead to the south, the Pogy Notch Trail continues around Upper South Branch Pond and eventually reaches Russell Pond. Turn left instead onto the Center Ridge Trail, which climbs steeply the next 2.1 miles to The Traveler's Peak of the Ridges.

You begin your ascent up a boulder pile with views opening up over Upper South Branch Pond. Meadowsweet, fireweed, and other dry-soil wildflowers grow among the boulders, softening the mountain's appearance but not the rugged climb. Unlike Katahdin and the other granite mountains in the south end of the park, The Traveler was created by a volcano that erupted 400 million years ago. The rock of The Traveler—and the Deadwater Mountains (see Hike 41, Horse Mountain)—is composed of rhyolite, which has a finer-grained, darker tan appearance than granite. Traces of iron in the rhyolite here have stained the rocks red. At 2.2 miles from Upper South Branch Pond, you top a cliff with a dramatic view of Pogy Notch and the South Branch ponds. Pinnacle Ridge is the sheer-faced ridge to the south. The North Traveler is across Howe Brook Valley to the north.

The trail rises less steeply for the next .5 mile, in and out of scrub birch and pine, sheep laurel, blueberries, bunchberry, and rock tripe. The last mile is a steep scree scramble with occasional brief levelings among dwarf birch, mountain ash, sheep laurel, reindeer moss, mountain cranberry, and Labrador tea.

At 3.6 miles, as you drag yourself to the 3,225-foot summit, notice the evidence around you that moose, also, frequent this peak. From Peak of the Ridges you might believe you could

The author on The Traveler

touch the sky. Views around you are breathtaking. To the east 1.5 miles away is the 3,541-foot trailless main summit of The Traveler, beyond which lie the park's eastern boundary and the East Branch of the Penobscot. North of you is North Traveler peak. West are two-peaked South Branch Mountain and Pogy North where Pogy Brook braids its way ten miles to Wassataquoik Stream and Russell Pond. To the south is South Traveler Peak.

Return by the same trails to South Branch Pond Campground.

The Traveler is barren as a result of the Great Wassataquoik Fire of 1903, which swept from north to south, funneling through Pogy Notch into the Russell Pond area. The fire burned every trace of life, even consuming topsoil. This makes climbing The Traveler difficult and slow, as every step must be well-placed. Allow plenty of time, and be cautious, especially over the scree, to avoid spraining an ankle on your descent.

Howe Brook

Total distance: 6 miles
Hiking time: 3 hours
Vertical rise: 700 feet
Maps: USGS 7.5' Wassataquoik Lake, The Traveler; USGS 15'
Traveler Mountain; Baxter Park Map

Howe Brook is a small mountain brook with pools and cascades near South Branch Pond Campground in Baxter State Park. The hike is a beautiful walk for a small amount of effort. From the Matagamon Gate, drive 7 miles west on the Park Perimeter Road and turn left

(south) down South Branch Pond Road, continuing 2.3 miles to South Branch Pond Campground. (This turn is 36 miles north of the Togue Pond Gate to Baxter Park.) Park your car at South Branch Pond Campground.

To reach the Howe Brook Trail, leave

The chutes and pools of Howe Brook

South Branch Pond on the Pogy Notch Trail, skirting Lower South Branch Pond. At .1 mile, pass on your left the North Traveler Peak Trail, which leads 2.6 miles to that summit (Hike 43). Continue, passing under the sheer North Ridge, and come out onto the flat land separating Upper and Lower South Branch ponds. This flat land is a delta of Howe Brook that has gradually filled in and changed South Branch Pond from one lake into two. The trail passes a canoe landing and turns left away from the pond, paralleling the left bank of Howe Brook. This brook is also called Dry Brook, because it filters down into the delta fifty yards before it enters Lower South Branch Pond. Only during spring high water is the brook visible all the way to the pond. The area where the brook flows out into South Branch Pond from underground is a good fishing spot for brook trout.

At 1 mile, you reach a trail junction. The Pogy Notch Trail turns right and crosses Howe Brook. You continue straight ahead on the Howe Brook Trail. The brook originates from a spring in The Traveler and flows down the valley between North Traveler and Center Ridge. Walk upstream .2 mile where the falls and pools begin. A series of chutes here is fun to slide through on a hot day. These pools and chutes can entertain me half a day. The water is always very *cold*. There are smaller pools of sun-warmed water for children to splash in. Farther up the trail are some well-polished potholes hollowed out by centuries of water-swirled gravel. The water in these pools is crystal clear and emerald-tinted in the deepest places.

After leaving the falls, you cross and recross the brook and then begin a gradual ascent. You'll notice several stumps of large white pines, old and rotting, victims of the 1903 and 1914 fires. The Great Wassataquoik Fire of 1903 swept this area clear of all life and of even the topsoil. These huge stumps are the only remains of the fire. The young woods are still open and sparse, but sandy-soil plants such as hawkweed, goldenrod, asters, and meadow rue have begun to flourish. This sunny openness, resulting from the fire, gives a sparkle to the water and a sense of freedom to the hike.

At 1.8 miles up the Howe Brook Trail, the trail forks into a final loop. Take the right fork, cross the brook, and climb a rough trail through a deep ravine until you pass a set of hidden, almost secret falls. They are step falls and flumes through dark woods. At 2 miles from the stream's outlet, you come to the bottom of a vertical cascade twenty-feet high falling into a small pool. The spruce at the head of Howe Brook are noted as being Baxter Park's only virgin timber (besides those in the Klondike) to escape the axes and fires of the nineteenth and twentieth centuries. In the upper reaches of the brook, where the virgin timber begins, I've found many bleached skulls and bones of moose. The beginning of Howe Brook is either the location of or the outwash place for many moose deaths. Their antlers are found in a different location in the park.

From here, the Howe Brook Trail climbs out of the ravine and loops left to rejoin the path you took out. Retrace Howe Brook Trail to the Pogy Notch Trail and then back to South Branch Pond Campground.

Both the falls at the end of this trail and the cascades and pools near its beginning are perfect lunch spots. This is one of my favorite hikes. I can easily spend a whole day on this trail and not even go to the end.

Aroostook County

AN INTRODUCTION TO HIKING
IN AROOSTOOK COUNTY

Aroostook County, referred to within the state as The County, is Maine's largest county in area, but smallest in population. Much of eastern Aroostook County is covered with potato farms, while the central and western parts are mostly forest. Most of the timberland is within an area designated as the North Maine Woods (NMW), a 2.5-million-acre tract of land that covers most of Aroostook and some of Somerset, Piscataquis, and Penobscot counties.

NMW is the administrative wing of the landowners of this area, mostly paper companies, and is responsible for managing public access for hunting, camping, canoeing, fishing, and hiking. Organized in the early 1970s, NMW checks people in and out at checkpoint gates and charges minimal fees for use of the land. This large section of Maine encompasses two entire river systems—the Allagash and the St. John—over 2,000 miles of permanently maintained gravel roads, dozens of campsites, and a system of gates, permits, and access control to prevent confusion and getting lost. For advance information, map, and camping permit, write to North Maine Woods, P.O. Box 421, Ashland, ME 04732-0421. It is also acceptable to register at the gate. Reservations are not taken.

The terrain and topography of Aroostook are different from the rest of the state. The area is largely a flat expanse of sedimentary shales, left fairly undisturbed by the mountain building that folded, warped, and changed the rest of Maine. It remains much the same as when Maine was laid down as sediment at the bottom of a shallow sea over a span of about fifty million years, during the Devonian period. Some variation in rock type and terrain occurs to the southeast, closer to the action that rumpled and peaked the rest of Maine. Some of these variations, namely the few mountains in The County, offer the best opportunities for views, both for fire wardens and for hikers.

The easiest hike to reach is Hedgehog Mountain, located beside ME 11 4 miles south of Winterville and 13 miles north of Portage. The trail begins at a picnic area on the west side of ME 11. The well-used 1½-mile trail leaves from the parking lot, passes the Maine Forest Service (MFS) ranger cabin, and rises easily to the 1594-foot summit, an elevation gain of 500 feet. Although the firetower has been removed, views are good south to Round and Peaked mountains, St. Froid Lake, Fish River Lake, and Portage Lake. To the northwest, Deboullie and Black mountains form twins.

In the Presque Isle area are two mountains of yellow rhyolite, the remains of volcanoes: Quaggy Joe and Haystack mountains. Both mountains offer easy hikes. Quaggy Joe, altitude 1213 feet, is located in Aroostook State Park. The 2¼-mile round-trip hike takes less than two hours, with an elevation gain of 600 feet. Of the twin peaks, South Peak is higher, but North Peak has better views: west to the cone of Haystack Mountain, with Chandler and Squapan behind. On a clear day, you can see the outline of Katahdin to the southwest.

Haystack Mountain, the other volcanic remnant, is located at the roadside of ME 163 halfway between Presque Isle and Ashland. The trail starts on the north side of the highway and is a short climb of less than a mile to the peaked summit. Even though in the shape of a volcano, Haystack is merely the eroded stump of a volcano that has been weathering away for hundreds of millions of years.

Two other hills can be climbed in the Presque Isle area—Mars Hill, half a mile from the New Brunswick border in the town of Mars Hill

Ten Hikes in Aroostook County

(south of Presque Isle on US 1), and Number Nine Mountain, 1638 feet in altitude with a firetower. Number Nine is accessible only by a four-wheel-drive vehicle. It is about 15 miles west of US 1 in Bridgewater.

A four-wheel-drive vehicle or a canoe is also necessary to reach the two hikes that follow. Priestly Mountain and Allagash Mountain (both actually in northern Piscataquis County) can both be hiked as side trips on a canoe trip of the Allagash Wilderness Waterway. Allagash Mountain, with its firetower, is located at the shore of Allagash Lake. Do not attempt to reach this mountain on logging roads; save it for the canoe trip. Priestly Mountain can be hiked from Umsaskis Lake on the Allagash Waterway, round trip of seven miles, or can be reached by four-wheel drive or a rugged vehicle, making the hike a four-mile round trip from the road. To reach the latter trailhead from Ashland, drive west on the American Realty Road to Six Mile Checkpoint, pay fees, and confirm directions to Priestly Mountain. Follow the Realty Road to the intersection of the Churchill Dam Road, 67 miles west of Ashland. From the intersection, it is 7.5 miles on the Churchill Dam Road to a small sign on a tree on the left indicating the trail. The trail follows an old road to Drake Brook, the outlet of Priestly Lake, which is nestled among low hills. Here the trail from Umsaskis Lake joins your trail for the ¾-mile climb to the 1900-foot summit.

Aroostook's two highest peaks, Peaked Mountain (2270 feet) and Round Mountain (slightly lower), stand two miles apart west of Ashland. A four-wheel-drive vehicle may be needed to reach these mountains. Round Mountain's firetower, presently not in operation, offers closeup views south to Peaked Mountain and northerly views of the northern Maine woods and waterways. The trail to Peaked Mountain is difficult to find and directions should be obtained at the MFS office in Portage. Then drive west from Ashland on the American Realty Road. Just beyond Six Mile Checkpoint, take the left fork and drive about 11 miles to the Machias River. Cross the river and turn right onto a logging road. At 5 miles from the river crossing, a road to the right takes you 5 miles to Round Mountain. Or, if you continue until you are 10 miles from the river, you will come to a trail on the right to Peaked Mountain. Neither of these trails should be attempted without updated information from Six Mile Checkpoint or from an MFS station, since the trails are not frequently cleared of brush.

If you are fortunate enough to have time to spend in Aroostook County, you might want to find out about some of the many interesting canoe trips on the Allagash, St. John, St. Croix, Aroostook, and Fish rivers. With a DeLorme Maine Atlas and Gazeteer, you should be able to find places to camp with a fireplace, picnic table, and tent site.

The one hike written in detail in this section, Deboullie Mountain, is in a state recreation area with plenty of campsites, fishing, hunting, and even sporting camps.

Deboullie Mountain

Total distance: 6 miles
Hiking time: 4 hours
Vertical rise: 850 feet
Maps: USGS 7.5' Deboullie Pond; USGS 15' Fish River Lake;
  North Maine Woods Map

Deboullie Mountain gets its name from the French past participle for "fallen," which refers to the fallen rock in the De-boullie Slide. It is the highest of a small cluster of mountains in the wilderness south of St. Francis on the New Brunswick border. Owned by the State of Maine in a 15,000-acre tract, the mountain is surrounded by Great North-ern and International Paper Company lands, whose roads provide the lengthy approach. This area is part of the North Maine Woods (NMW), explained in the introduction to Aroostook County.

The approach to the hike, or combina-tion canoe paddle and hike, begins in St. Francis on ME 161 between Fort Kent and Allagash. From the St. Francis Post Office, drive 5.9 miles southwest on ME 161 to Chamberlain's Market on the left. (This is also 22.6 miles southwest of the junction of ME 11 and ME 161 in Fort Kent.) Beside the market, the Pel-letier Brook (Negro Brook) Road leaves ME 161 for the North Maine Woods. At .1 mile, fork right, leaving Pelletier Brook Road on the Red River-Togue Pond Road, and at 7.5 miles, check in at the gate, pay an entry fee, and obtain a *North Maine Woods Map of Roads and*

Campsites. At 8 miles fork right, and at 8.5 miles fork left, following signs to Red River Camps. At 15.3 miles, you pass on the right NMW Togue Pond Camp-site. Park off the road at 19.3 miles, by a sign that reads, "This road dead ends at Red River Camps." You may first want to visit the attractive Red River Camps, owned and run by Chris and Pete Norris, who can confirm trail in-structions and rent you a canoe or camp. Return to the dead-end sign to begin the hike.

If you are starting by canoe, put in at Pushineer Pond below the dead-end sign, follow the right (east) shoreline through the thoroughfare into Deboullie Pond, and canoe two-thirds of De-boullie's right (north) shoreline, past a rock slide to a break in the alders lead-ing to a campsite. The mountain trail leaves behind the campsite at a sign, 1 mile to the tower.

If you are hiking all the way, walk northeast down to the old dam between Pushineer Pond and the Red River. Wade across the river or walk over the old dam, skirting NMW Pushineer Pond Campsite on the left, and continue walk-ing the woods road. At .4 mile, pass on your left NMW Thoroughfare Campsite, and at .5 mile, pass on your left NMW Deboullie Campsite (no sign). From all three campsites you can see the tower on Deboullie's summit. At .8 mile, look carefully on your right for the remains of a rotting, abandoned boat, and shortly on your left is a small abandoned dump with a wooden sign that says "tower." The trail leaves from behind the dump, follows the shore of Deboullie Pond, and crosses the Deboullie Slide, where lichen-patched rocks are sprinkled with spears of fireweed, making a green and pink color combination in August. There is a place in the Deboullie Slide called the "ice chest," where the ice never melts, even in summer. The trail stays near shore beyond the slide until shortly, at 2 miles, it runs into a campsite with a sign to the tower.

The last mile leaves the rear of the

Deboullie Slide at base of Deboullie Mountain, on the shore of Deboullie Pond

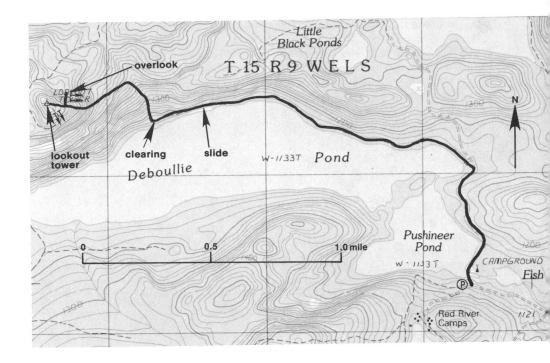

campsite and climbs steeply west up the mountain. Halfway up, avoid a right fork, and ascend through large birches and maples. At .3 mile from the summit, pass a spring on your left and then a spring on your right (both have good water). The trail then climbs very steeply through spinulose wood fern, wild sarsaparilla, wood sorrel, bunchberry, clintonia lily, and asters. Just before you reach the summit, a short trail on your right leads to a view of Black Mountain. One last effort brings you to the open summit, with fire warden's cabin, fire tower, and helicopter launch pad. Mountain ash decorates the dooryard with white flowers in spring and red-orange berries in summer and fall.

Views from the tower stretch south to Katahdin and north to New Brunswick. Northeast, the sheer cliffs of Black

Mountain drop into Little Black Pond with Black Pond behind. In the distance, you can see Eagle Lake and Square Lake. Eastward lie Deboullie Pond, Pushineer Pond, and St. Froid Lake. Southeast, behind Fish River Lake and Portage Lake, are Haystack and Squapan mountains near Presque Isle. South-southeast, Whitman and Chapman mountains, named after the original owners of Red River Camps, hide the camps on Island Pond. South, behind these mountains, Round and Peaked mountains are Aroostook County's two highest. Southwest beyond Gardner Pond is Gardner Mountain, beyond it to the right is Togue Pond, and in the distance is Long Lake. South-southwest are the Rocky Brook Mountains, of which Horseshoe Mountain with its tower is the highest. Deboullie's ridge continues northwest over Fifth Negro Brook.

Return by the same trail to your car. I had a startling experience while gazing from the tower ladder one afternoon. A Maine Forest Service helicopter landed on a launch pad a dozen yards away, bringing fire warden Marilyn Kenyon to work. The warden's cabin was as unusual as her transportation to work: the windows were boarded to keep out bears. Although the tower is not currently in operation, it is maintained so it can be reopened at a moment's notice.

Bemis Mountain and Elephant Mountain Loop

Time allowed: 2 days, 1 night
Total distance: 18 miles
Vertical rise: 2,900 feet
Maps: USGS 7.5' Metallak Mountain, Hougton; USGS 15'
  Rangeley, Oquossoc; MATC 7 (1988)

Bemis Mountain and Bemis Stream valley offer striking beauty in the heart of the western Maine mountains between Rumford and Oquossoc in the Rangeley Lakes region. This 18-mile backpacking circuit covers rugged ground, especially on the first day's ascent of the four main summits of Bemis Mountain. The Elephant Mountain lean-to, located at the far end of the circuit, makes a good place to stop over in spring or fall. In midsummer, however, you should carry a tent or plan to sleep on the ground in case the lean-to is filled. The seven-mile exposed ridge of Bemis Mountain is not the place to be in bad weather.

To get to the trailhead, drive north on ME 17 from Rumford toward Oquossoc. At 26 miles, look carefully for the Appalachian Trail (AT) crossing at a scenic turnout at Height of the Land, 11 miles south of Oquossoc. From here you can see the long, many-peaked open ridge of Bemis Mountain falling into the vast spread of Mooselookmeguntic Lake. Backtrack .6 mile to the Bemis Valley Trail (former AT), and park in a gravel pit across the road (east side) from the Bemis Valley trailhead. This is where your trip will begin and end.

Day 1: Height of Land to Elephant Mountain

Total distance: 8 miles
Hiking time: 8 hours
Vertical rise: 2,750 feet

Begin with a full canteen. From the Bemis Valley Trail walk .6 mile north on ME 17 to the AT crossing at Height of the Land. (To the right the AT goes east to Four Ponds Mountain and Sabbathday Pond—Hike 7.) Hike mileage begins where the AT crosses ME 17. Follow the white blazes left (west), dropping straight down to Bemis Stream for .8 mile. Cross the stream on a footbridge and ascend to a dirt road, which used to be the Rumford and Rangeley Lakes Railroad bed. (From here, it is one mile north on the road to the southeast shore of Mooselookmeguntic Lake.)

Follow the AT across the road and very steeply up the northeast shoulder of Bemis Mountain. At 1.2 miles, a spring is the last sure water for the entire Bemis Ridge. The next .5 mile will find you grabbing trees and pulling yourself up a very steep trail, but by the time you have gone 1.6 miles, the most difficult ascent is over. Leave the woods

and ascend over ledges to the first of many knobs or false summits. There are five false (apparent) summits, but only three are named: First, Second, and Third. The "Fourth" (really the sixth) is not a false summit but the actual one. Cross a ravine and rise over quartz-swirled granite through blueberries to the "First" summit of Bemis Ridge at 2,604 feet at 2.2 miles.

Follow cairns and white blazes past clumps of juniper, sheep laurel, and cranberries. At 3.1 miles you come to the "Second" summit of Bemis Ridge at 2,923 feet. Cross more ledges with increasingly beautiful views north to Mooselookmeguntic Lake, east to Height of the Land, and west toward the rest of the Bemis summits. At 4.6 miles, in a small sag, you come to Bemis Mountain lean-to, built in 1988. This spot with its nearby spring is a good place to eat lunch and rest from the strenuous assault of Bemis Mountain.

Continue to the "Third" summit, 3,110 feet high, at 5 miles. Blueberries, bunchberries, reindeer lichen, and other lichens garnish the exposed trail here and there. After descending into another sag, the trail climbs at 6.3 miles to the "Fourth" and, at 3,532 feet, the highest summit. It has two knobs. At this point you have completed all but 150 feet of the vertical rise for the entire two-day trip.

Views are outstanding south to Elephant Mountain and Old Blue Mountain (Hike 6); west to Metallak Mountain, which rises over the Richardson Lakes; northwest to Aziscoos Mountain (left) (Hike 9) and Observatory Mountain (right); north to Bald Mountain (Hike 8) over Mooselookmeguntic Lake, and behind to Cupsuptic Lake; north-northeast to Rangeley Lake; northeast to Saddleback Mountain (Hike 11); and south-

east to Tumbledown (Hike 2) and the Jacksons (Hike 3).

From the summit, begin a steady descent onto the long connecting ridge between Bemis and Elephant Mountains. You are likely to see spruce partridge along the trail and possibly partridge (ruffed grouse). At 7.3 miles the AT comes to a junction with the Bemis Stream Trail, which runs 6 miles back to ME 17 where you parked. Turn left onto the Bemis Stream Trail, following blue blazes from now on. A half mile from the trail junction, you cross the headwaters of Bemis Stream and soon reach the Elephant Mountain lean-to at 7.9 miles. This is a good place to spend the night; however, be prepared to sleep on the ground if the lean-to is filled. The lean-to is at the edge of a shallow bog grown up with laurel. There is a spring for water, or you can backtrack to Bemis Stream. (Stream water should be either boiled for one minute or filtered.) You are five miles from the closest dirt road here and should not be bothered by sounds of civilization.

Day 2: Elephant Mountain to ME 17

Total distance: 10 miles
Hiking time: 5 hours
Vertical rise: 150 feet

From the Elephant Mountain lean-to you will return to ME 17 by the Bemis Valley Trail, which follows Bemis Stream. However, a worthwhile side trip of up to 4 miles round trip (included in the mileage listed above), will take you through a magnificent primeval forest of lofty virgin red spruce. The red spruce stand is also accessible to the Old Blue hike (Hike 6). From the Elephant Mountain lean-to, follow the former AT southwest in the direction of Old Blue Mountain.

View to Bemis Mountain from the summit of Old Blue

This 2-mile side trip will take you through a forest of virgin red spruce, an awe-inspiring sight. Some of the trees date back to the early 1600s. When your trail intersects the present AT (white blazes) and the Clearwater Brook Trail (blue blazes), turn around and retrace the 2 miles to the Elephant Mountain lean-to.

The six-mile Bemis Valley Trail is blue-blazed and can be picked up across the bog from the lean-to. Follow the blue blazes carefully, as recent logging has confused the trail a bit. Dense evergreens begin to open into sunny mixed woods as the trail crosses and recrosses Bemis Stream from time to time. Look for wildlife (deer, raccoon, bear) along this trail.

The trail descends gently into predominantly birch woods with various kinds of hardwood ground cover: Canada mayflower, bunchberry, clintonia lily, wild sarsaparilla, wood sorrel (*Oxalis*), and doll's-eye (white baneberry). The trail follows old lumber roads for short sections and slabs a steep bank above the stream.

The last crossing of Bemis Stream, where the widening stream tumbles through boulders, is a good place for lunch. The trail then continues on the other side of the stream, ascends a high bank leaving the stream, and descends through raspberries to a logging road. Turn right on the logging road, walk .2 mile, and follow the trail left back into the woods a short distance until you cross another dirt road. This is the old railroad bed that you crossed yesterday.

Continue in the woods for the last mile, rising gently from Bemis Valley to ME 17. The last mile has been relocated through recent logging slash and is not scenic at present. The trail ends at Bemis Stream on ME 17 where you parked your car.

Crocker Peaks and Sugarloaf

Time allowed: 2 days, 1 night
Total distance: 12.6 miles
Vertical rise: 6,300 feet
Maps: USGS 15' Stratton; MATC 6 (1988)

Between Kingfield and Stratton and south of Flagstaff Lake stand three of Maine's twelve "four-thousand-footers": Sugarloaf, North Crocker, and South Crocker. Sugarloaf, at 4,237 feet, is Maine's second highest mountain. The Crockers are close behind: North Crocker is 4,168 feet, and South Crocker is 4,010 feet. The Crockers are separated by a deep col, and Sugarloaf is separated from the Crockers by the Carrabassett River Valley, so there are tremendous gains and losses of elevation for hikers. For this reason, the trip is divided into two days of climbing. Rugged terrain, dramatic views, and the hand of nature make the trip very rewarding.

Hiking the three peaks almost makes a circuit. To end where you began requires 4.5 miles of road walking (not included in the distance of the hike). By spotting a second car at the hike's end at Sugarloaf Ski Lodge, you can avoid the road walk, however. You can reach the Sugarloaf lodge (in Carrabassett Valley) by driving 15.4 miles north of the center of Kingfield on ME 27, or 8 miles south of the junction of ME 16 and ME 27 in Stratton. Turn south off ME 27 at the "Sugarloaf USA" sign and drive 2 miles to the lodge parking lot.

The beginning of the hike is further north on ME 27 at the Appalachian Trail (AT) crossing, 19 miles north of Kingfield, 2.5 miles north of the Sugarloaf road, and 5.3 miles south of the junction of ME 16 and ME 27 in Stratton. A parking area marks the trailhead.

Day 1: ME 27 to Crocker Cirque

Total distance: 7.3 miles
Hiking time: 6 hours
Vertical rise: 4,200 feet

Begin with a full canteen of water. From the parking area on the southwest side of ME 27, begin following white AT blazes south on the 5-mile gradual approach to North Crocker Peak. The trail passes through a low area of large white and yellow birches, climbing on an even grade toward the north-south ridge that makes up the Crocker Peaks. At 1.4 miles, you mount the first of several knobs of North Crocker Ridge. The trail levels for a short distance and then rises gently for another mile.

With the elevation, the woods change gradually from predominantly white and yellow birches to predominantly spruce and balsam. Spruce grouse inhabit the upper reaches, bold birds that do not

0   0.5   1.0 mile

N

T 4 R 2 B K P W K R
(CROCKERTOWN)

A South

Day 1

North
Crocker
Mtn.

Crocker
Mtn

South

South
Crocker
Mtn.

Bigelow

Carrabassett

JEEP TRAIL

Branch

South

Day 2

Sugarloaf
Ski Lodge

Sugarloaf
Mtn

Sugarloaf Side
Trail to the
Summit

RAILROAD

OLD

BM
1548

run from people. This trait gives them the nickname "fool's hen" and has made necessary a law to protect them from hunting. They can be distinguished from ruffed grouse by their darker plumage and red eye markings.

At 4 miles the trail crosses a small tributary to Stoney Brook, not always reliable and the last water for 3 miles. The .8-mile ascent from here is very steep to the crest of North Crocker's summit. The trail has eroded, exposing roots of trees that will eventually die. At the crest of North Crocker summit, turn southeast. A short walk brings you to the partially wooded summit of 4,168 feet. Views are limited to a glimpse northeast to Bigelow through the trees.

The trail descends steeply .5 mile into the col between the peaks, levels briefly to cross the sag, and then shoots up .5 mile to South Crocker Peak. When the trail reaches its high point on South Crocker, a short blue-blazed side trail leads 50 yards to the right to a rocky outcrop at the 4,010-foot summit. Views are limited, but to the south you can see Spaulding Mountain with Mount Abraham (Hike 12) behind.

Return to the AT and begin descending the east shoulder of South Crocker .5 mile to a small intermittent spring. Shortly, at a rock opening, the trail opens, swings off the shoulder, and plummets steeply toward Caribou Valley and down to the floor of a glacial cirque between the two Crocker peaks. Be careful; the descent is steep and rocky.

A cirque is formed when a glacier cuts down from the top of a ridge, carving a large round hollow with a vertical rounded headwall. Crocker Cirque has an unusual added feature. Beavers have dammed a small tributary to the South Branch of the Carrabassett, flooding the cirque floor into a pond, which reflects the cirque walls bordering it. A quiet

morning or evening can be spent in this sanctuary, watching birds, beaver, and clouds mirrored from high above the cirque walls.

At the floor of the cirque, a blue-blazed side trail leads left past the beaver pond .2 mile to Crocker Cirque campsite. You will find here a wooden tent platform and one improved tent site, but no lean-to. The brook has plenty of water, which should be boiled or filtered.

Day 2: Crocker Cirque to Sugarloaf Lodge

Total distance: 5.3 miles
Hiking time: 4½ hours
Vertical rise: 2,100 feet

Follow the blue-blazed side trail from Crocker Cirque campsite back to the AT. Turn left on the AT and begin a 1-mile descent to the South Branch of the Carrabassett. Soon after you start, you pass a small beaver pond on the right and descend gradually through white birch with numerous wildflowers beneath: wild sarsaparilla, Canada mayflower, purple wake-robin, and starflower. At .9 mile, cross Caribou Valley Road. This gravel road ends 2 miles south (right) at Caribou Pond. It is a good exit route north (left) 4.5 miles to ME 27, if you are unable to complete the climb of Sugarloaf.

At 1 mile, cross the South Branch of the Carrabassett, quite a large mountain brook. In high water, the stream can be difficult to cross. You may need a stick for balance, and you may have to remove boots and pants. Running shoes make stream crossings less painful. They dry quickly and are much lighter to carry than sneakers. On the other side, the trail runs upstream for a short distance and then climbs away to the

Crocker Peaks viewed by skiers on Sugarloaf

southeast, ascending Sugarloaf's steep western spur through birch and poplar. The trail opens and sends you scrambling up a series of slate ledges. Climbing is slow in this steepest section. At 1.7 miles, you reach the rim of Sugarloaf's vast glacial cirque and begin skirting the rim on a precipitous trail to the top of the cirque headwall. This is a dramatic stretch of trail.

At 2 miles, the trail sees you safely back into woods of well-spaced, beautifully shaped spruce in small alpine meadows. The trail levels for .5 mile, a welcome respite. At 2.6 miles, cross a small mountain brook (last water), and at 2.8 miles, you reach the Sugarloaf Summit Side Trail. Leave the AT and follow blue blazes left uphill for .5 mile to Sugarloaf's 4,237-foot summit. This was the route of the AT before it was rerouted

away from the developed summit. Now it is relatively unused, and you are likely to see spruce partridge and other wildlife. The .5-mile spurt to the top does not seem as steep as earlier ascents of the day. (Knowing it is your last ascent helps it seem easier.) With this last elevation gain, growth reduces from spruce-pine to scrub spruce-pine, to blueberries and bunchberry, and finally to lichen-splotched black scree at the pointed bare summit.

A few buildings on top might detract from your feeling of isolation, but you will never have any more dramatic views than from the summit of Sugarloaf. The peak is small, giving the feeling that you can almost jump off in any direction. Most of the other four-thousand-footers in Maine are close around, and Bigelow looks as if you can touch it. Due south is Spaulding Mountain with Mount Abraham (Hike 12) behind. Southwest over Redington Pond are Poplar Ridge, Saddleback Junior, Saddleback (Hike 11), and the Horn. Far in the distance, Mount Washington in New Hampshire is visible on a clear day. West are the Crocker Peaks with Crocker Cirque between. North are the many peaks of the seventeen-mile Bigelow Range, left to right: Cranberry Peak (Hike 15), the Horns, West Peak (Hike 13), Avery Peak, and Little Bigelow (Hike 14). Behind Bigelow due north is Coburn Mountain (Hike 20). North-northeast behind Little Bigelow are Little and Big Spencer mountains (Hike 31), with Big Squaw (Hike 27) to the right. Northeast is the Barren-Chairback Range, behind which you can see Katahdin on a clear day. To the east rises the barren cone of Burnt Hill.

Notice the very dark rocks at the summit. Sugarloaf is made of Devonian gabbro and ultramafic rock. Gabbro is formed when molten magma wells up from the earth's interior like an underground "blister"—the same way in which granite is made. Whereas granite is light-colored because of its particular mineral content, gabbro is very dark or black since it contains dark feldspars, amphiboles, and other mafic minerals. Sugarloaf was created in the Devonian period, which dates it at 350 to 390 million years old. It was a much larger formation back in those days, but erosion has gradually worn it down to a fraction of its former size.

The old AT used to cross over the summit and descend to the northwest, dropping away from the gondola station. In winter this is a ski trail. The old AT is no longer blazed or maintained and is not advised for a descent.

The ski lifts and gondola descend the north side of Sugarloaf. Choose a ski trail and walk down a very steep 2 miles to Sugarloaf Lodge. From the open slope you can watch Bigelow your entire descent to the lodge where you spotted a car. If you did not spot a car, walk 2 miles out to ME 27, turn left, and walk the remaining 2.5 miles to the AT crossing where you parked at the trailhead. This adds 4.5 miles and 2½ hours to the hike.

Webster Lake Trail

Time allowed: 3 days, 2 nights
Total distance: 22 miles
Vertical rise: 1,000 feet
Maps: USGS 7.5' Trout Brook Mountain, Frost Pond, Webster
  Lake; USGS 15' Telos Lake, Traveler Mountain; Baxter Park
  Map

The Webster Lake hike in the northern wilderness of Baxter State Park begins at Trout Brook Farm Campground, 2.6 miles west of the Matagamon Gate entrance from Patten. (For driving directions, see the Baxter Park introduction.) You are not likely to see many people on this trail, and wildlife is abundant. This is the only trail through the extensive northern wilderness of the park, featuring Matagamon Lake to the northeast and Webster Lake to the northwest. You will find solitude and silence in this little-explored lake country.

This 22-mile trail—among streams, brooks, ponds, and bogs—is often wet and muddy. Rain chaps and waterproof boots could enhance your hiking. In the mud on the trail you can count the tracks of numerous animals: moose, deer, coyote, bobcat, raccoon, and some very large bear.

The first 14.6 miles of the hike follows the old Freezeout Trail, and the last 7.2 miles, the Webster Lake Trail. The hike ends on the Park Perimeter Road, 8.5 miles west of Trout Brook Farm at the Webster Lake Trail sign at Black Brook Farm. A car should be spotted here in

advance, because walking back to Trout Brook Farm would add 8.5 miles to the hike, for a total of 30.5 miles.

Water is plentiful along the way. I have seen bear tracks along this trail, so packs should be hung in trees at night.

Day 1: Trout Brook Farm to Little East Branch

Total distance: 6 miles
Hiking time: 3 hours
Vertical rise: 180 feet

This is a half-day hike, which allows you some driving time to the park before setting out on the trail. Leave the Park Perimeter Road at the Freezeout Trail sign at Trout Brook Farm Campground, following the dirt road down to Trout Brook. Behind you to the south is a view of Trout Brook Mountain. At .4 mile you reach a foot bridge at Trout Brook. Cross the bridge and begin walking the old road in a northwesterly direction. The Freezeout Road provided winter access to Webster Brook. Logs were hauled and stored along this road. At "freezeout" time in spring, soon after

Webster Stream Lean-to

East Branch Lean-to

Freezeout Trail

Day 1

thaw, high water carried logs downstream.

At .6 mile, you enter a field (now being reclaimed by alders and beautifully shaped spruce) with meadow flowers such as goldenrod, pearly everlasting, and fireweed. This field was part of the old Trout Brook Farm Operation, run by a succession of companies from 1837 to the early 1950s and based at the campground. At one time there were barns, blacksmith shops, storage houses, and quarters for crews. The camp was destroyed by fire three times. Old foundations can be seen in the fields and in the campground. The operation harvested timber south and west of Matagamon Lake. Logs were then driven into Matagamon Lake and down the East Branch of the Penobscot.

At the far end of the old field, follow tire tracks into the woods. This is the old "Burma Road," abandoned about 1950 and named for its ups and downs as it crosses a series of slate ridges. At 1.5 miles, you cross two branches of Boody Brook. In autumn, the entire trail is lined with large, colorful mushrooms, puffballs, and bracket fungi. At 3.3 miles you cross Frost Pond Brook, where the trail begins to level out. At 3.5 miles, the trail swings close to the shore of Second Matagamon Lake by an extensive spread of sawdust. The trail skirts the lakeshore for the next 2.3 miles, cutting around a cove and across two brooks, the second of which is Hinckley Brook.

At 5.4 miles, you cross a raspberry clearing on the lakeshore. (An overgrown branch of the old Freezeout Road used to enter this clearing from the left.) A clear, cold spring on the left of the trail provides good water. At 5.6 miles, an obscure trail forks left away from the lakeshore, but you should bear right, staying next to the lake. In another .3 mile you reach a small clearing on

Webster Brook. (The Burma Road used to cross the stream here.) The trail turns sharply left off the tote road and onto a woods trail by Little East Branch lean-to on the shore of the stream.

The lean-to accommodates three, and there is room for tenting in the vicinity. Webster Stream lean-to is 2.5 miles further on, but in a less scenic location. Little East Branch lean-to is more open (important during bug season) and has a view of the confluence of Webster Brook and the smaller East Branch of the Penobscot.

Day 2: Little East Branch to Webster Lake

Total distance: 7.8 miles
Hiking time: 5 hours
Vertical rise: 380 feet

From Little East Branch lean-to, the trail turns west and trends west-southwest all day, dipping down to Webster Brook and back. The old Freezeout Trail has been made more scenic by side trails that run along the stream bank, so when you come to forks, always choose the right fork along the stream.

At .8 mile you come to Grand Pitch, the largest falls on Webster Brook. At the falls, Webster Brook narrows into oblique walls of slate, forcing a great volume of water through a narrow gorge. Above the falls, the stream is quiet flatwater. A rusted old sign on a tree here reads, "Many friends regret the death of Joe Howell, killed here by an explosion of dynamite, April 1, 1912." Webster Brook and Webster Lake were yet another watercourse used for log driving from Telos and Chamberlain lakes. Originally, these lakes flowed north through the Allagash River into the St. John and into Canada. To avoid paying taxes to Canada, in 1841 lumber

Grand Pitch on Webster Brook

companies blasted the Telos Cut through the narrow piece of land between Telos and Webster lakes and built Churchill Dam on Heron Lake (part of Chamberlain Lake). This reversed the flow of water, from north to south, and logs could be driven more directly and less expensively to Bangor by way of the Penobscot.

The trail turns away from Grand Pitch and back into the woods. Along the shore, vegetation is lush: cedars, alders, spruce, balsam, hardwoods, mosses, polypody ferns, and mushrooms. One mile before Indian Carry, the trail crosses the red-blazed town line from T6 R9 to T6 R10. After passing several small clearings it arrives at 2.3 miles at Webster Stream lean-to at Indian Carry. Indian Carry was recorded by Thoreau in *The Maine Woods* as a place where Indians carried their canoes around rapids, but the lean-to is situated on a quiet bend in Webster Brook. The

woods here are a mixture of young hardwoods, with typical hardwood floor vegetation—starflower, long beech fern, wood sorrel, bunchberry, clintonia lily, Canada mayflower, Indian cucumber, and trillium. Here and there ancient rotting stumps stand witness to the huge white pines that once covered the state and burned in the great fire of 1903.

At 5 miles, you cross a field growing up in raspberries. At 6.3 miles you cross Hudson Brook, and at 7.8 miles a side trail leads to the Ice Wagon Campsite. At 8.7 miles you pass the outlet of Webster Lake and take a side trail to the Webster Lake outlet campsite, a beautiful place to pitch your tent (no lean-to). Lake water should be boiled one minute before drinking, cooking, or washing dishes. Beyond the campsite you'll find the remains of an old lumberman's dam and the Webster Lake outlet into Webster Stream. On his 1857 canoe trip through Moosehead, the Allagash, and return by Webster Stream and the East Branch of the Penobscot, Thoreau ate lunch at this outlet. While his Indian guide searched for navigable waters on Webster Stream, Thoreau and his companion proceeded on an old path on the south side of the stream. From the campsite you can see an island, with a campsite which can be reached by canoe. (Canoes are not provided.) You will probably see loons floating on the lake and perhaps eat a supper of brook trout.

Day 3: Webster Lake to Black Brook Farm

Total distance: 8.2 miles
Hiking time: 4 hours
Vertical rise: 420 feet

Leave Webster Lake outlet and skirt the east shore (no views) on the Freezeout Trail. At .9 mile, you reach the junction with the Webster Lake Trail. At this junction, an old tote road runs west (right), past Boathouse Campsite near the shore, beyond Baxter Park boundary to the west end of the lake, and upstream

along the Telos Cut to Telos Dam and Telos Lake. Bear left onto the Webster Lake Trail. From here it is 7.2 miles to the end of the trail at Black Brook Farm. The mileage count for today begins here, in keeping with other trail guides for the Webster Lake Trail. The trail here, often wet, parallels Thissell Brook upstream, passing near Thissell Bog.

At 2.1 miles (3 miles from Webster Lake outlet campsite), you pass through the clearing of an old lumber camp built in 1947. The woods on this trail are generally bigger and older than those on the Freezeout Trail. At 3.4 miles cross a small brook that flows northeast into Wadleigh Bog; at 5.3 miles rise over a burned area now growing with sheep laurel, bracken fern, trailing arbutus, reindeer lichen, and young well-shaped spruce and pine. At 6.8 miles, cross the town line and walk .5 mile to the end of the trail at Black Brook Farm. This was an outlying camp of the Trout Brook Farm Operation.

If you have not spotted a car at Black Brook Farm, you must turn left and hike back to Trout Brook Farm, adding 8.5 miles and three hours to your trip.

50

Russell Pond

Time allowed: 5 days, 4 nights
Total distance: 40 miles
Vertical rise: 3,200 feet
Maps: USGS 7.5' Mount Katahdin, Katahdin Lake, The
*   Traveler, Wassataquoik Lake; USGS 15' Katahdin, Traveler*
*   Mountain; Baxter Park Map*

One of the nicest vacations an out-door lover can plan is a few days at Russell Pond in Baxter State Park. The hike-in campground is eight miles from the nearest road and situated among many fascinating geological and natural wonders. This backpacking trip requires that you carry your backpack 8 miles to Russell Pond on the first day and 8 miles back out on the last day. Since you will be camping at Russell Pond each night, the three intervening days will be spent on short day trips. You should be in good physical condition before attempting this trip. Children also need to be experienced and strong. My four year old made this trip with a few rest stops along the way, but I doubt that many children his age could have enjoyed it.

No one may visit Russell Pond without reservations, which are obtained by writing and sending fees to Baxter Park Headquarters, 64 Balsam Drive, Millinocket, ME 04462. See the introduction to Baxter State Park in this guidebook for general driving directions to the park and for more information on hiking and backpacking in Baxter.

The facilities at Russell Pond were originally built early in the twentieth century for an outlying logging camp of the Draper Operations and were later converted into six sporting camps. Of the six, the kitchen-and-dining cabin is the only one that remains, and it is now used as a bunkhouse. There are also lean-tos and tent sites available for reservation.

The trail to Russell Pond begins at Roaring Brook Campground, which you can reach by entering the Togue Pond Gate, the southeastern entrance of Baxter State Park. Bear right at the fork and drive approximately 8 miles to the end of the road at Roaring Brook Campground.

Day 1: To Russell Pond

Total distance: 8 miles
Hiking time: 5 hours
Vertical rise: 400 feet

Get an early start from Roaring Brook Campground. The latest departure time allowed is 1 P.M.; after that the rangers close the trail. (You may have to spend the previous night there.) Even though the Russell Pond Trail remains in a valley and there is very little vertical rise, your pack is always heaviest on the first day. After signing in on the list in the Roaring Brook ranger's cabin, follow the trail to the junction of the Chimney Pond Trail (left). Stay to the right on the Russell Pond Trail and cross Roaring Brook on a bridge. In 50 yards the Russell Pond Trail turns sharply left. (Ahead is Sandy Stream Pond Trail, which rejoins the Russell Pond Trail 1 mile farther north.) Notice the decaying cavities of huge stumps of white pine, the remains of forest fires and logging that occurred earlier in this century. You ascend through large mixed hardwoods and cross a spring-fed brook.

In 1 mile, the Sandy Stream Pond Trail comes in on the right. About .2 mile beyond you begin skirting the east shore of the first Whidden Pond, passing on the left a short side trail that leads to its shore. Here is your best view on the trail, looking west into Katahdin's three great cirques: the Great Basin, the North Basin, and the Northwest Basin.

The trail soon bears northeast away from the pond and flanks South Turner Mountain. You then descend to the South Branch of Wassataquoik Stream, which the trail follows onto an old tote road to a junction. Here the Russell Pond Trail turns left and leaves the tote road. In times of high water you should follow this trail. In drier weather, the more interesting route is the Tracy Horse Trail (tote road) to the right, described here. You continue down the tote road along the South Branch of the Wassataquoik approximately 3 miles, where it flows into the main current of Wassataquoik Stream. Here you must ford the main stream; this can be dangerous in high water, especially with a pack. Running shoes make crossing the stream easier than with bare feet. These shoes dry quickly and are much lighter to carry than sneakers. Two Wassataquoik Stream lean-tos are located on the south shore at the ford; this is the site of the former South Branch Dam. An old lumber camp called the Bell Camps was located here on the south shore where the lean-tos are. One hundred yards north of lean-to #2, blue blazes lead you to an old but occupied beaver pond. The grass-grown dam still supports water, and beaver still live in the lodge, which is now covered with wildflowers.

After fording the stream, you pick up the old Wassataquoik Tote Road west across Turner Brook, through some old fields. In July and August you will be slowed by the bountiful blueberry bushes lining the trail. If you're quiet, you might even see a bear feasting on them. Raspberries are also abundant in the sunny fields in July and August. In the years from 1910 to 1914 these fields were cleared for a lumbering town called New City, population 800, part of the Draper Operations of which Russell Pond was an outpost. A careful look through the waist-high brush will reveal rusting implements from the town's sawmill, store, and houses. There was even a hotel in New City.

The Tracy Horse Trail returns you to the Russell Pond Trail .4 mile from Russell Pond. Turn right and cross Turner Brook on a bridge. In .3 mile the Northwest Basin Trail comes in on the left, and shortly you arrive at Russell Pond Campground.

Day 2: Grand Falls and Lookout Ledges

Total distance: 7 miles
Hiking time: 4 hours
Vertical rise: 500 feet

You can find plenty to do at Russell Pond without ever leaving the area. Fly-fishing brings many people in. Canoes rent by the hour: for floating, paddling around, fishing, and moose-watching. In fact you can often see several moose on the pond at one time. The pond itself does not afford pleasant swimming, because it is too shallow and the bottom is too soft. But you can backtrack on the Russell Pond Trail .1 mile to the Northwest Basin Trail and follow it to the right a few hundred yards to Turner Deadwater, a pleasant and warm swimming place. For a colder swim, jump into Wassataquoik Stream, south or east of Russell Pond.

If you'd like to plan a more strenuous day, try one or both of the following hikes. Each takes no more than a couple of hours. Both leave from the Russell Pond shore opposite the lean-tos: the Lookout Ledges are 1.3 miles away, and the Grand Falls on the Wassataquoik are 2.7 miles off. The start for both destinations is the same. Walk .4 mile around the west and north shores of Russell Pond until you reach the junction where the Lookout Ledges Trail turns left and the Grand Falls Trail bears right.

Grand Falls. From the junction, follow the Grand Falls trail east through widely spaced evergreen growth, a result of forest fires in 1884 and 1903. In blueberry season, plan on taking longer than normal to hike this trail. The trail turns and leaves Russell Pond, skirting Bell Pond, where a curious beaver may swim beside you the pond's entire length. At 2.2 miles you cross a beaver flowage and walk on logs through a marsh up through tremendous boulders rolled by glaciers and onto the old Wassataquoik Tote Road. When you come to a large cairn, be careful. (At this point, a short trail leads right 25 yards through alders to Inscription Rock, a granite boulder at the edge of the stream bearing the worn inscription "Tracy and Love commenced operation on Wassataquoik, Oct. 16, 1883.") Turn left at the cairn and follow the stream. Shortly, at 2.5 miles, the trail leaves the tote road and climbs the stream's high bank. The next .2 mile offers dramatic views down into the gorge of the churning rapids and pitches of Grand Falls.

The Grand Falls Trail ends 2.7 miles from Russell Pond on a high ledge overhanging the lower end of the falls fifty feet below. The falls are a series of swirling drops rather than one large one. You can see several washed-out potholes on the opposite shore. The trail ends at the falls, from which you retrace your trail to Russell Pond. It is possible to bushwhack .7 mile further downstream to the site of Old City. To do this, leave the trail at 2.5 miles on the old tote road, and pay close attention, since below this point it is overgrown.

Old City, located at the fork of Pogy Brook and the Wassataquoik, was the first lumber camp within the present park boundaries. It was settled in 1883 by the Tracy and Love Operation and burned in the Great Wassataquoik Fire of 1903. This intense fire, fed by slash from lumbering operations, roared down through Pogy Notch and fanned out around Russell Pond. The fierce heat burned down through the humus, and the fire burned over 132 square miles, leaving effects visible today north and east of Russell Pond. Giant stumps stand in memory of the thousands of virgin white pines that burned. On most of the Grand Falls Trail, trees are spaced widely, and today, over eighty-five years later, the soil is only just beginning to support larger trees. This accounts for the acres of blueberries and sheep laurel along the trail.

On your return, .2 mile from Grand Falls, where the trail dips low along the stream, you can make your way down to the water and ford the stream to a smooth granite terrace on the opposite side. Here the stream eddies into a sizeable swimming hole—a perfect place to picnic and swim, with blueberries and cranberries for dessert. This is also the site of former Mammoth Dam, part of the Tracy and Love Operation.

Lookout Ledges. The Lookout Ledges Trail takes you to open ledges on a small hill north of Russell Pond. (There is no water on the trail.) You ascend easily from the junction with the trail to Grand Falls. About .7 mile along this trail, you cross open ledges with fine views east and south down over Bell Ponds and the Grand Falls Trail. Continue to the 1,730-foot summit ledges, where the panorama includes a large part of the interior of Baxter Park.

To your left (north) you can see the clustered conical peaks of South Traveler, behind them, The Traveler (Hikes 43–44) and on its left flank, Pinnacle Ridge. These peaks are remnants of a volcano 400 million years old. (Tucked behind The Traveler lie South Branch ponds in the northern end of the park.) Northeast is lower South Traveler, and east in the distance lies Mount Chase, the roots of an older volcano of 500 million years ago. Sable Mountain is the lower ridge in front of Mount Chase. Southeast over Bell Ponds rises the scree-splotched granite summit of North Turner, with South Turner (Hike 32) behind, both on the eastern border of the park. To the south behind Russell Mountain rises Katahdin (Hikes 33 and 34), Maine's highest mountain, whose Pamola Peak and Knife Edge rise behind the Howe (North) peaks. This is a most unusual aspect of Katahdin—different from any views from locations you can reach by car. Southwest you can see the outlet of Russell Pond.

Return to Russell Pond the way you came, turning right at the junction with Grand Falls Trail. The many huge decaying stumps illustrate the size of the gigantic white pines that grew in the area before the fires of 1884 and 1903.

Day 3: Wassataquoik Lake and Green Falls

Total distance: 6.4 miles
Hiking time: 4 hours
Vertical rise: 300 feet

This is a lengthy day hike that offers swimming possibilities in good weather. You should carry a lunch, but water is available at Green Falls. From Russell Pond Campground walk north behind the lean-tos, and turn left behind lean-to #4 through a raspberry patch on the Wassataquoik Lake Trail. From the clearing you enter spruce-fir woods on a wide, easy trail of blueberries and bunchberry. At .7 mile, a short side trail takes you to Deep Pond, where Russell Pond campers may use a park canoe.

At 1.3 miles, you climb and pass an arm of one of the Six Ponds, where you can usually see a moose. A park canoe is chained to a tree at the pond, and you can borrow the key from the Russell Pond ranger. Shortly you cross first a causeway formed by a glacial esker between two of the ponds and then the connector stream between the ponds. At 2.1 miles you cross Turner Brook, the outlet of Wassataquoik Lake. Soon after, the trail descends to the shore of beautiful Wassataquoik Lake.

Another canoe is locked on this shore for the use of Russell Pond campers. If you have borrowed the key from the Russell Pond ranger, you may want to canoe around the lake. At the lower end

Crossing Wassataquoik Stream

of the lake is a small island with a cabin and campsite for which reservations can be made. The lake, 1.5-miles long and .7 mile at its widest, is remarkable for many reasons: its gravel beaches and firm bottom make for good swimming, and tall peaks surround the crystal clear water, which is emerald green because of its 200-foot depth.

If you continue hiking, the trail follows the south shoreline. Rock-hopping in and out along the undulating shore is slow-going, but rewarding for an observer of nature.

Halfway down the south shore of Wassataquoik Lake, at 3.2 miles from Russell Pond, you cross a stream flowing into the lake, and 25 yards beyond, a blue post marks a side trail that leads .1 mile to the left to Green Falls. This waterfall, unlike showy Ledge Falls and Katahdin Falls, is named Green Falls because it flows like angel hair over a backdrop of emerald green moss.

Above the beautiful lower falls, you can climb to the upper falls, which flows through a deep cleft in the rock. At the upper falls are good views across the lake to South Pogy Mountain, with its talus slope (rock fall). Water from the falls is potable.

Return to Russell Pond the way you came.

Day 4: Davis Pond

Total distance: 11 miles
Hiking time: 7 hours
Vertical rise: 1,600 feet

This rugged hike will take you to Davis Pond in the Northwest Basin and back. Do not attempt it if you are tired or have blisters. You will be hiking all day, so pack a lunch and some snacks.

Leave Russell Pond Campground on the Russell Pond Trail and bear southwest .1 mile to a junction, where you turn right onto the Northwest Basin Trail and cross the outlet of Turner Deadwater on the remains of an old lumbering dam. At 1.2 miles, you reach a junction with the North Peaks Trail. Stay on the Northwest Basin Trail, and at 2.6 miles, cross Annis Brook where another outlying camp of the Draper Operation was once located. Many logging implements can be found on the forest floor in this area. In another .5 mile you'll ford a branch of the Wassataquoik and continue on or near the stream through shady conifers. You'll cross the Wassataquoik again at 3.7 miles and continue along the banks of its tributary, Northwest Basin Brook.

This is a wonderful walk. For nearly 1 mile everywhere you look there are pools, falls, and huge boulders. The farther you go, the smaller and more beautiful the brook becomes. At 4.6 miles, you walk along the edge of the smooth brook bed of polished rock for 50 yards. From here you begin the steep ascent into the Northwest Basin, following the headwaters of the brook up steps of rock.

At 5 miles you reach an open knoll at Lake Cowles (elevation 2,850 feet) with excellent views. Nearby is a large stone pile marking an old survey line called the Monument Line, surveyed through the United States east to west in 1833. Lake Cowles is a large tarn, typical of ponds formed in the floors of glacial cirques. The trail crosses the lake outlet and skirts the northeast end of the lake through knee-high sheep laurel, a pink garden in July. Beyond, you climb an unusual heath-covered knoll sixty-feet high, a miniature glacial "sheepback" or roche moutonnée. There are also two smaller ones in this basin. Descend over the far side of the sheepback, and at 5.3 miles you reach Davis Pond lean-to. An overnight stop here can be prearranged with the Russell Pond ranger. To the left is a short trail leading down through the sheep laurel to clear little Davis Pond, nestled in a corner of the basin under the cliffs of Harvey Ridge. Beneath the few feet of water in the pond, moose tracks crisscross the bottom. To your left stands another sheepback, smaller than the one at Lake Cowles. You can sometimes see a tiny waterfall threading down from the top of the basin wall. I once stayed overnight in this lean-to during a terrific thunderstorm but felt cozy and protected by the high walls of the basin. You can swim in Davis Pond, but don't let the hours slip by. You have to leave in plenty of time to retrace your route to Russell Pond.

Day 5: Back to Roaring Brook

Total distance: 8 miles
Hiking time: 5 hours
Vertical rise: 400 feet

Today is the day you leave Russell Pond. But there are many things to do if you can stay longer, such as bushwhack up Russell Mountain or Tip-top Mountain. Either of these treks can make a day or half-day hike and should be discussed with the ranger at Russell Pond for best directions. Neither hike's mileage or directions are included here.

Russell Mountain is one of the two northern extremities of Katahdin known to early loggers as the "Black Hills." From the Wassataquoik Valley it is the highest peak visible, at 2,801 feet. It is trailless and may be bushwhacked from the Russell Pond Trail with directions from the ranger.

Tip-top is the westernmost of the two northern spurs of Katahdin. On its north slope you can still find the remains of two old sluices used in the Draper Operations of 1910–1914. They are best reached by bushwhacking from the Northwest Basin Trail near Annis Brook. High on Tip-top are the ruins of an old lumber camp, as well as a very small pond.

For your departure from Russell Pond, take the Russell Pond Trail and Tracy Horse Trail back to Roaring Brook the way you came in.

Regardless of how much hiking you do at Russell Pond, you can't help but enjoy just being there. Nothing can surpass a long summer evening's paddle around the pond. Views from the pond include North Turner Mountain to the southeast, with South Turner behind; south to Russell Mountain and lower Tip-top, backed by the Howe (North) peaks of Katahdin. Southwest is three-peaked Mullen Mountain; west is Wassataquoik Mountain. To the north lie South and North Pogy mountains, and the ridge to the east leads to the Lookout Ledges.

On a summer evening at Russell Pond I watch moose come in to feed until there are five or six in sight, grazing underwater and raising up to munch and watch. I see an evening's hatch of mayflies and the joyful looks breaking over the faces of the fly fishermen on shore and in canoes. A mother otter leads her two babies on an evening swim. A cedar waxwing darts 30 yards after a bug, and then catches and eats it. As the sun sets I watch North Turner Mountain turn reddish-pink to purple and then darken in the dusk, as I slowly paddle to shore. On the walk back to my lean-to in the quiet evening I glimpse the last of the chipmunks and evening grosbeaks.

I can recall one August night, lying on the canoe dock until midnight watching the annual August meteor shower located in and around the Constellation Cassiopeia. The only competition was from fireflies in the dark night.

Guidebooks from The Countryman Press and Backcountry Publications

Written for people of all ages and experience, these popular and carefully prepared books feature detailed trail and tour directions, notes on points of interest and natural phenomena, maps and photographs.

Walks and Rambles Series
Walks and Rambles on the Delmarva Peninsula, $8.95
Walks and Rambles in Rhode Island, $8.95
Walks and Rambles in Westchester (NY) and Fairfield (CT) Counties, $7.95

Biking Series
25 Mountain Bike Tours in Vermont, $9.95
25 Bicycle Tours on Delmarva, $8.95
25 Bicycle Tours in Eastern Pennsylvania, $8.95
20 Bicycle Tours in the Finger Lakes, $7.95
25 Bicycle Tours in the Hudson Valley, $9.95
25 Bicycle Tours in Maine, $8.95
25 Bicycle Tours in New Hampshire, $7.95
25 Bicycle Tours in New Jersey, $8.95
20 Bicycle Tours in and around New York City, $7.95
25 Bicycle Tours in Vermont, $8.95

Canoeing Series
Canoe Camping Vermont and New Hampshire Rivers, $7.95
Canoeing Central New York, $10.95
Canoeing Massachusetts, Rhode Island and Connecticut, $7.95

Hiking Series
50 Hikes in the Adirondacks, $10.95
50 Hikes in Central New York, $9.95
50 Hikes in Central Pennsylvania, $9.95
50 Hikes in Connecticut, $9.95
50 Hikes in Eastern Pennsylvania, $10.95
50 Hikes in the Hudson Valley, $9.95
50 Hikes in Massachusetts, $9.95
50 More Hikes in New Hampshire, $9.95

50 Hikes in New Jersey, $10.95
50 Hikes in Northern Maine, $10.95
50 Hikes in Southern Maine, $10.95
50 Hikes in Vermont, 3rd edition, $9.95
50 Hikes in West Virginia, $9.95
50 Hikes in Western Pennsylvania, $9.95
50 Hikes in the White Mountains, $9.95

Adirondack Series
Discover the Adirondack High Peaks $14.95 (available July 1989)
Discover the Central Adirondacks $8.95
Discover the Eastern Adirondacks $9.95
Discover the Northeastern Adirondacks $9.95
Discover the Northern Adirondacks $10.95
Discover the Northwestern Adirondacks $10.95 (available November 1989)
Discover the South Central Adirondacks $8.95
Discover the Southeastern Adirondacks $8.95
Discover the Southern Adirondacks $9.95
Discover the Southwestern Adirondacks $9.95
Discover the West Central Adirondacks $13.95

Ski-Touring Series
25 Ski Tours in Central New York $7.95
25 Ski Tours in New Hampshire $8.95

Other Guides
Maine: An Explorer's Guide (revised edition available spring 1989) $14.95
New England's Special Places $10.95
New York State's Special Places, $12.95
The Other Massachusetts: An Explorer's Guide $12.95
State Parks and Campgrounds in Northern New York $9.95
Vermont: An Explorer's Guide, 3rd edition, $14.95

The above titles are available at bookstores and at certain sporting goods stores or may be ordered directly from the publisher. For complete descriptions of these and other guides, write: The Countryman Press, P.O. Box 175, Woodstock, VT 05091.